UNDERCURRE

TRAVELLERS AND IRELAND: WHOSE COUNTRY, WHOSE HISTORY?

UNDERCURRENTS

Published titles in the series

Facing the Unemployment Crisis in Ireland by Kieran Kennedy

Divorce in Ireland: Who Should Bear the Cost? by Peter Ward

Crime and Crisis in Ireland: Justice by Illusion? by Caroline Fennell

The Hidden Tradition: Feminism, Women and Nationalism in Ireland by Carol Coulter

Managing the EU Structural Funds by Alan Matthews

Diverse Communities: The Evolution of Lesbian and Gay Politics in Ireland by Kieran Rose

Democracy Blindfolded: The Case for a Freedom of Information Act in Ireland by Patrick Smyth and Ronan Brady

Ireland: The Emigrant Nursery and the World Economy by Jim Mac Laughlin

Test-Tube Mothers: New Reproductive Technology in Ireland by Susan Ryan Sheridan

UNDERCURRENTS Series Editor Fintan O'Toole

Travellers and Ireland: Whose Country, Whose History?

JIM MAC LAUGHLIN

CORK UNIVERSITY PRESS

First published in 1995 by
Cork University Press
University College
Cork
Ireland

British Library Cataloguing in Publication Data

A CIP catalogue record for this book is available from the British Library

ISBN 1 85918 094 9

Typeset in Ireland by Seton Music Graphics Ltd, Co. Cork
Printed in Ireland by ColourBooks, Baldoyle, Co. Dublin

Contents

Acknowledgments

Thanks to Ethel Crowley who first raised the idea that I should get involved in the Traveller issue and who shared so many of the ideas discussed here; Anne Doherty, Chrissie O'Sullivan and Brian Ó Gallachóir of the Cork Traveller Visibility Group who introduced me to the present-day concerns of Irish Travellers and whose intellectual integrity has truly been a source of inspiration; Mick Murphy, cartographer at UCC for graphs and diagrams; and Fintan O'Toole for encouraging a study of the Irish Travellers.

INTRODUCTION

There have been three important watersheds in the evolution of Irish Traveller society since the mid-nineteenth century. The first occurred during the nation-building, latter half of the century and it witnessed the denigration of nomadism in bourgeois nationalist discourse. The latter insisted that the values of property owners, specifically those of the rural petty bourgeoisie, were to be hegemonic and that Travellers had no place in modern Ireland. This meant at best that Travellers were treated as an historical anachronism, one that hopefully would not constitute too strong a blemish on the face of Mother Ireland as she struggled for recognition in the international community of developed nations. However, Traveller-settler relations at this time were also marked by more tolerance than they are now. They were also characterised by a higher degree of deference than now in that Travellers were considered simply as one part of 'the poor that you always have with you' and treated as part-time wards of church-based charitable institutions. It should be stressed that Travellers at this stage were only partially dependent upon charity and that they still carved out a living for themselves by moving out and into the formal economy of rural Ireland where, as 'tinkers', they often managed to find social acceptance and a modicum of material subsistence.

The second watershed began around the 1960s when, like so many other rural Irish people, Travellers moved off the land and relocated in cities, especially in Dublin, Cork, Limerick, Derry, Belfast and Galway. This study shows that the move to the cities presented Travellers with more problems than opportunities. It undoubtedly showed the resilience of Traveller society as more and more Travellers shifted into new niches in the urban economy and carved out a living for themselves in increasingly hostile and competitive urban environments. However, Travellers also experienced a high degree of structural discrimination at this time. The world that they had formerly occupied was now literally reconstructed and buried under the powerful infrastructural changes that were considered 'developments' for the national society but clearly were 'maldevelopments' for Travelling communities. Their traditional halting sites disappeared under a barrage of road 'improvement' schemes and the very occupations that once linked Travellers to settled society were becoming increasingly redundant in a consumer society where 'pound shops' and plastic did away with so many Traveller ways of making a living. Travellers, and the long-term urban unemployed, now became increasingly dependent upon the welfare state in this period. Like other inner-city communities, Travellers also witnessed a growing despondency and an overdependence upon the welfare state for survival.

The third watershed in the evolution of Irish Traveller society began with the late 1980s. This is the period that Travellers are still struggling through. It is marked by significant new developments as well as many worrying set-backs. It has seen the setting up of a Task Force which, under the political leadership of Liz Mc Manus, has witnessed a prioritisation of Traveller needs and interests. It has also seen President Mary Robinson openly encouraging a greater awareness of Traveller ethnicity and recognising the role of grass-roots Traveller communities in building a place for Travellers in contemporary Irish society. This period is now witnessing the introduction of new legislation that will make it illegal for business premises and public houses to discriminate against Travellers by keeping these premises 'Traveller Free'. This is a very important legislative development for Irish Travellers. It will undoubtedly see Travellers taking the issue of anti-Traveller discrimination to the courts and making the new legislation a living reality rather than an empty piece of legislative reform.

More importantly still, however, this period has witnessed the emergence of an ethnic intelligentsia among the Travellers themselves. This has contributed to the growth of an articulate new leadership capable of voicing Traveller concerns and capable also of raising the political consciousness of travelling people. This is probably the most significant development in Traveller society this century. The struggles of these grass-roots leaders deserve far more support from non-Travellers than they have hitherto received. This is all the more important in the light of two important set-backs in the evolution of Traveller society. The first of these has seen the rise of a virulent anti-Traveller racism here which has clear parallels with anti-immigrant racism in mainland Europe. This has meant that Traveller communities, particularly those living outside the large Traveller ghettos in the Greater Dublin area, are now more exposed to vigilante attacks than they ever were before. As a result of the emergence of what are little short of Ku-Klux-Klan-type delegations that are not averse to employing the tactics of urban gangs, isolated Traveller families in many parts of this country are now literally living in fear for their lives.

The second important set-back in Traveller culture is the gradual internalisation of feelings of social inferiority among Travellers themselves. Having been oppressed and demoralised for so long, a growing body of evidence suggests that many Travellers are beginning to internalise feelings of racial inferiority and taking to alcohol abuse and petty crime as outlets for the frustration they experience in their day-to-day lives. Turning the tide on this downward spiral of depression and alienation will require all the energies that Traveller support groups can muster. It will also require far greater support from the more progressive elements in Irish society, and far more space where Travellers, local residents, farmers and property-owners can sit down and discuss their very real grievances.

This study is divided into four sections. Chapter One looks at the denigration of nomadism and the prioritisation of sedentarism in Western social sciences from the late seventeenth century to the nineteenth century. Chapter Two follows with an account of the racialisation of Travellers as a result of the rise of bourgeois nationalism and nation-building in the late nineteenth century. The third chapter focuses on developments in Irish Traveller society between 1960 and the late 1980s. This is followed by a discussion of anti-Traveller racism and the geography of closure, both of which are seeking to force Travellers out of Irish towns and villages into the very 'Traveller-ghettos' where so many of their problems originate.

1. A People Without a History, Without a Homeland?

The romanticisation and denigration of nomadism

In his *Muqaddiman*, or 'Universal History', the fourteenth-century Islamic scholar Ibn Khaldoun, surveying human development from the nomadic perspective concluded that nomadic societies were:

> . . . closer to being good than settled peoples because they are closer to the first State and are more removed from all the evil habits that have infected the hearts of settlers[1].

He also developed an aesthetics of progress which suggested that societies declined, morally as well as physically, the more sedentary they became. The rigours of nomadism, he argued, preceded the softness of settled life, particularly the settled life of urban dwellers. For Ibn Khaldoun the desert was the great reservoir of civilization. He also suggested that nomadic peoples had an advantage over settlers because they were 'more abstemious, freer, braver, healthier, less bloated, less craven, less liable to submit, and altogether easier to cure'.[2]

Irish Travellers have recently been expressing similar sentiments and many of them regard the travelling life as healthier and preferable to life on the dole in disadvantaged urban areas. As one Traveller from Coolock, County Dublin stated:

> I'd sooner be travelling anytime, I would sooner be gone out of here this minute now, with a good wagon and a good pony or something you know. I would be

> more used to it. See you can't stick these houses. You would want to be doing something in them, like out in the country, or doing something.[3]

Another Traveller, Missie Collins from Finglas, said:

> Well I'd like to be out travelling, if there was schooling and good facilities, like toilets and electricity, and to get it all without hassle. I would, I'd sooner be out travelling, yeah – I would. *Because it's freer, I think you feel better like the old people. They're healthier, but now that you are stuck in one place, it's sicker that they're getting, since they moved off the road. I think it's healthier on the road than it is now.*[4] (Emphasis added)

Such romanticisations of the travelling life are rare today. However, Bruce Chatwin was one writer who also idealised nomadism and travelling cultures, going so far as to suggest that nomadism was more natural than sedentarism. Criticising the assumption that sedentarism and nomadism were mutually exclusive, he argued that:

> Nomad and farmer are linked to a common past and, to some extent, share common aspirations. If the nomad recovered the mobility of former times, he was also committed to an ideology of growth. The cleavage deprived the farmer of rich sources of animal protein and the nomad of essential grain. Nomad and farmer might hate each other, yet they needed each other.[5]

Stressing the nomadic nature of much medieval life, he noted that 'progress' in late feudal England meant a 'journey', specifically a seasonal journey of the king round the castles of his barons; of bishops round their dioceses; of nomadic shepherds and 'hurds' round their pastures, and of pilgrims round a sequence of shrines.[6]

This latter practice was common in some parts of Ireland well into the twentieth century and was known as a 'turas'. Chatwin goes even further than Khaldoun in his romanticisation of nomadic societies. He shows how the Tibetan definition of 'human being', 'a-Gro ba', or 'a go-er', prioritises the nomadic over the sedentary. This is also true of Arab society where the 'true' Arab, the 'bedu', is a 'dweller in tents' as opposed to a 'hazar' – 'one who lives in a house'.

In Europe the exoticisation of Gypsies and the nomadic Romany reached new heights during the Romantic era. It is particularly evident in Prosper Merimee's novel *Carmen* and in Bizet's opera of the same name. In *Carmen* the Gypsy woman is an exotic 'other' who is the opposite to the staid Victorian image of womanhood. She is twinned with mystery and the supernatural and is unfaithful to her soldier lover, the representative of order, respectability and control. She suffers the consequences of her infidelity, being killed by a vengeful husband. Such romanticisations of Gypsies and nomads, common in Oriental and Western *fiction* in the nineteenth century, are in sharp contrast to the vilification of nomadic peoples and travelling cultures in Western *society*. They are also at variance with the denigration of nomadism in Western social sciences since the Enlightenment. Nevertheless, a yearning for a heroic nomadic past was a feature of a number of European peoples in the eighteenth and nineteenth centuries. Indeed, Anthony Smith has noted a specific nostalgia associated with nomadic lifestyles which embodies a hankering for a lost past, particularly on the part of sedentarised nomads. He argues that this nostalgia:

> . . . may focus on the desert steppes or plains, on forests or mountains, the cradle of the community or the seat of its halcyon days. It may induce a desire to return to a homeland that has been lost, or a passionate attachment to the homeland that has been forged after migration. It may attach a community to its former,

> or adopted life-style, more firmly than before when it was routinely accepted, and so help to differentiate the community more sharply from its neighbours.[7]

He further distinguishes between two categories of nostalgia, that of kinship and that of territory. Some societies, he argues, evince a yearning for their 'lost clan organization and the semi-nomadic, simple life-style of their ancestors which a sedentarised and, perhaps, more urbanised civilization has eroded'.[8] Most nationalities, however, not least those of nineteenth-century western Europe, prioritised territorial communities over tribal communities based on ideas of kinship and filial loyalty. In more extreme cases they exorcised tribalism and nomadism from their national psyche, and from their nationalist history. Their longing for a primitive past was focused on a particular local terrain which acted as the arena for their communal polities and formed the basis of their territorial identities. The point to note here is that, among some European peoples at least, strong territorial attachments by no means precluded a sense of feudal or clan pedigree rooted in a nomadic past. Normans, Anglo-Saxons, Franks and Visigoths have all formed strong nation-states and this has not obscured their nomadic or feudal origins. Neither has it prevented them from 'romancing' their nomadic past.

In yet other societies, including post-colonial nations as far apart as Ireland and Algeria, attachment to a nomadic past, or to tribal and clan pedigrees, was seen as a political embarrassment, an obstacle to modernisation. As such it was something to be exorcised rather than revered. This was also the case in many Middle-Eastern, African and Asian countries in the post-colonial period, many of which had preserved strong traditions of nomadism right up to the late nineteenth century. Indeed, in many of these countries the twentieth-century push for modernity not only caused nomadism and sedentarism to be presented in oppositional terms – it also led to a marginalisation of nomadic groups and a prioritisation of propertied interests – such that the concerns of nomadic groups were interpreted as inimical to national progress. As we shall presently see, this has been particularly true of Ireland since the late eighteenth century. Here, as elsewhere in Europe, the trauma of 'settling down' – involving as it did the appropriation and privatisation of property, and the adoption of petty bourgeois sedentary life-styles by the natives – often operated in such a way as to separate sedentary from nomadic people. It also separated sedentary peoples from their nomadic past and severed any links still existing between nomadic communities and bourgeois society. Thus did cultural nationalists and the bourgeoisie of nation-building Europe dissociate themselves from the wretched of the European earth. This contributed to the racial denigration of Travellers and Gypsies and caused them to be located outside the national body politic. These groups were considered to be racially inferior to propertied classes because they had no stake in the nation-state or its making. They were 'outcasts' who constituted what to all intents and purposes could be classified as Europe's 'untouchable' class. The sections that follow discuss the origins of Irish Travellers and the problems inherent in definitions of Travellers. These are issues which are not only of academic interest but also influence our perceptions of Travelling people and their position in modern Irish society.

DEFINING TRAVELLERS: THE PECULIARITIES OF THE IRISH CONTEXT

Given the pejorativisation of nomadism, and the exclusion of Travelling people from nationalist history and political discourse throughout the nineteenth century, it is not surprising that the problem of defining Travellers in Ireland, as in other European societies, is almost as elusive as Travellers themselves. Indeed, this problem of definition has been exacerbated by the fact that Irish 'tinkers' or Travellers were not only written out of Irish history and excluded from Irish society – they were also perceived as people without either history or a homeland. These were serious deficiencies indeed in a country where an ethnically-defined people, in their search for political recognition and respectability in the international community, were laying claim to national territory and justifying that claim partly on the basis that their historical pedigree was not tainted with racial inferiority through association with nomadism and Travelling people. Neglect of the nomad and the racialisation of Travellers were not just features of nationalist historiography in nineteenth-century Ireland. Travellers and Gypsies have long been buried beneath Western social and political discourse. This has allowed Europe to forget what has actually been done to Travellers, and to ignore what Acton calls 'the forgotten genocide at the heart of the European unconscious'.[9]

As far back as the ancient Greeks and Romans, Western philosophers have been contributing to this racialisation of nomadic communities. Even today Travellers and Gypsies scarcely feature, either as social categories or as communities in their own right, in the theoretical constructs of 'hard' social sciences like sociology, political economy and social psychology. Their informal economies are totally ignored by most students, despite the accessibility of these informal economies and despite also the fact that the informal economies of nomadic communities and Travelling people throughout Europe have been closely linked to the formal economies of feudal and bourgeois society since well before the fourteenth century. Excluded from nationalist history of individual countries, Travellers and Gypsies at the European level have been treated as exotic 'others' by 'soft' social sciences like anthropology and ethnography. At best they were a cultural curiosity, an incongruous social residue from a pre-modern past, a people to be paternalistically admired for their determination to remain doggedly true to an unconventional lifestyle in a rapidly changing and increasingly materialistic and 'settled' world. At other times their habitats were seen as 'beds of incest, whoredom, adulteries and of all the other black and deeply-damned impieties . . .

where grew the cursed tree of blasphemy and where are written all the books of blasphemies'.[10]

Drawing distinctions between Travellers and the 'settled' population in a peripheral society like Ireland is complicated by three factors. In the first place, colonial 'settlers' were almost synonymous with the settled population in colonial Ireland, and colonial conquest caused massive 'shake-outs' within the indigenous population. This meant that entire sections of the native population fell through the ranks of the class structure and often ended up among nomadic and traditional vagrant groups. However, unlike Elizabethan England where the enclosure system also transformed entire sections of the rural poor into 'sturdy beggars' and 'vagrants', those forced from relatively prestigious positions in Gaelic Ireland into vagrancy and mendicancy in colonial Ireland often retained the respect of the native dispossessed well into the eighteenth century. This meant that, from a purely materialist perspective at least, there was often a very thin divide separating 'settlers' from the 'dispossessed' and 'Travellers' in colonial Ireland.

The second reason why it is so difficult to clearly distinguish between the 'settled' population and 'Travellers' in nineteenth- and early twentieth-century Ireland is because large sections of the so-called 'settled' population were extremely mobile. This was particularly true of the rural poor. As an 'emigrant nursery', Ireland has been linked to the outer edges of an expanding world economy from at least the seventeenth century.[11] Indeed, in the nineteenth century large numbers of young adults from small farming and working-class backgrounds were raised alongside well-established 'emigrant trails' that led to Britain, the United States, Canada, Australia and South Africa. They also forged new trails to the expanding frontiers of the world economy and literally 'peopled' its outer edges from the mid-nineteenth century onwards. Similarly, in sending cash 'remittances' back home, the emigrant sons and daughters of urban and rural Ireland contributed to the very survival of small farming and working-class communities traditionally serviced by Travellers well into the twentieth century. The 'Scottish money', or 'emigrant remittances', which such 'seasonal migrants' sent home accounted for as much as twenty per cent of the cash income of poor families in impoverished areas throughout the west and north-west of Ireland, right up to the eve of World War I.[12]

Finally, in the late nineteenth century very large numbers of migrant workers were moving between Ireland and mainland Britain and these were often indistinguishable from conventional Travellers or 'tinkers'. Handley has estimated that almost 38,000 of these 'seasonal migrants' were annually moving between Ireland and England in the closing decades of the century.[13] Many of these engaged in 'tattie-hoking' and other unskilled harvest work and their destinations reflected a need to locate in regions accessible to the rural poor, including poor 'tinkers' and Travellers. Many of the former would have been indistinguishable from the latter, and may all in fact have been considered as 'tinkers' by their Scottish and English employers. Many more 'settled' seasonal migrants may have regarded seasonal work in lowland Scotland or the north of England simply as a geographical extension of 'hiring out' practices that were customary among impoverished rural and working-class families throughout late nineteenth-century Ireland. Such poor families 'hired out' children, some of them as young as ten years of age, to local farmers and other employers in an effort to supplement meagre family incomes in districts where opportunities for paid employment for adults were few and far between. Their poverty, and their survival strategies, tended to identify them with, rather than distinguish them from, 'tinkers' who similarly looked on the 'travelling life' as a strategy for survival that was infinitely preferable to the impoverishment of rural sedentarism.[14]

Rao has defined Irish Travellers as 'endogamous nomads who are largely non-primary producers or extractors, and whose principal resources are constituted by other human populations'.[15] This definition circumvents many of the problems confronted in categorisations of Travellers in class-divided societies with large subaltern groups, such as those of nineteenth-and early twentieth-century Ireland. Firstly, it classifies Travellers as nomads living within territorially-bound societies who have no territorial claims on the country they inhabit. It emphasises the 'outcastness' of Irish Travellers from 'settled' society, even though some sections of the Travelling population opted for the settled life in order to survive, and even though large numbers of the 'settled' population were in fact highly mobile in a social and geographical sense. Secondly, in stressing their 'outcastness', this definition also emphasises the disjuncture between Traveller communities and the host nation. Thus, although Irish Travellers have had clear links with 'settled' society for many centuries, they were apart from, and not part of, either the 'settler' colonial society or the organic nation that Irish nationalists sought to construct. Thirdly, in emphasising the fact that Irish Travellers are endogamous nomads, Rao allows us to distinguish between Travellers and exogenous New Age Travellers and migrant workers, even where the latter are as impoverished as, and sometimes more impoverished than, Travellers. In so doing, he avoids economic reductionist categorisations of Travellers as the 'eternally poor' and focuses instead on the cult of nomadism as a defining feature of Irish Travellers. Finally, in stressing the fact that the principal resources of Irish Travellers are constituted by other groups, notably the rural, middle-class and working-class communities which Irish Travellers service, Rao emphasises the functional links between 'settled' and Traveller communities. Thus he allows Travellers to have distinctive social and economic functions, as well as a distinctive and often extremely dynamic social and economic structure.

IRISH TRAVELLERS AND THE ORIGINS QUESTION

Ní Shuinear has correctly argued that the discourse on the origins of Irish Travellers is dominated by 'the unspoken assumption that the validity of Gypsy/Traveller culture is up for definition and approval by the majority population'.[16] No such assumptions are made about other minority cultures. For Ní Shuinear indeed, the origins debate is 'a smokescreen', a diversion which prevents us from addressing the pragmatic questions surrounding the position of Travellers in contemporary Irish society. Acton has gone even further than this and argued that the proper response to the origins debate is to deconstruct the necessity of defining Irish Travellers in terms of their differences from settled society in Ireland.[17]

Both these writers show that nomadism and Traveller communities have been deeply embedded in European and Indian society since at least the fifth century. However, Irish Travellers are quite distinct from Gypsies and Romanies. It is well-established that the latter entered Europe from India, whereas Gypsies are thought to be of strictly Celtic origin.[18] Unlike Gypsies and Romanies, Irish Travellers are an endogenous, as opposed to an exogenous, social group and they have a far narrower geographical range than their European counterparts. Aside from small groups of Travellers of Irish descent in Europe and the United States, they are almost totally confined to Ireland and Britain. This means that their geographical imagination is correspondingly narrower than that of Gypsies and Romanies, many of whom range across Europe and penetrate into the Middle East.

When Gypsies and Romanies migrated from India through Persia and into Europe between the fifth and thirteenth centuries, 'commercialised nomadism' was a vibrant and acceptable feature of the medieval economy.[19] Soothsayers, magicians and sorcerers entered Europe via Asia Minor from India early in the ninth century. This was followed in the tenth century by another major migration of nomadic peoples from India, many of whom settled in the Balkan states. Others migrated across Europe to arrive in significant numbers in England and Scotland early in the sixteenth century.

Astrology, witchcraft, magical healing and divination were taken seriously in pre-Reformation Europe and were closely associated with, but by no means exclusive to, Travelling communities and Gypsies. The decline of magic and the rise of religion dealt a serious set-back to many of these communities. Thomas has shown that the decline of magic in Europe can be connected with the growth of urban living, the rise of science and the spread of self-help ideologies.[20] All of this emancipated large sections of European society, especially urban Europe, from a reliance on soothsayers and magical beliefs. It toppled many Gypsies and Romanies from the strategic positions that they formerly occupied in pre-Renaissance Europe. The demonisation of nomadic peoples both in Europe and India also coincided with the emergence of capitalism, the collapse and disintegration of feudalism in Europe, the collapse of the Asiatic mode of production in India and the progressive modernisation of these societies. It increased with the development of Indian capitalism and with the emergence of colonial rule from the eighteenth century onwards. Victimisation of Gypsies in European society generally coincided with periods of recession. It also occurred during the tortuous transition from feudalism to capitalism, during the Black Death and throughout prolonged periods of famine and economic depression. At such times, national, ethnic and religious xenophobic scapegoating of exogenous minorities and endogenous nomadic peoples reached new heights. 'Outsiders' like Jews and Muslims, and Travelling peoples like Romanies and Gypsies suffered more than most as a result of this. In the case of Ireland, the radical disavowal of 'tinkers' and Travellers probably occurred much later than elsewhere in western Europe. It was particularly exacerbated by the decimation of plebeian agrarian society from the late nineteenth century onwards and by the growth of a bourgeois Irish nationalism and clericalism after the Famine. Thus in Ireland, as elsewhere in nineteenth-century Europe, discrimination and suspicion followed Travellers and 'tinkers', but unlike most European countries where Gypsies were considered 'outsiders', in Ireland discrimination was practised by the settled Irish on the indigenous travelling Irish. This not only influenced popular perceptions of Traveller culture – often causing it to go underground – it also often forced Travellers to fit into the host society by taking on its customs and religious beliefs, thus discarding many of their own. In Ireland, France, Spain and Portugal, Travelling people adopted Catholicism as a protective move, though they often preserved a separate 'hidden' ethnicity and belief system underneath their public image.

Those engaged in 'commercialised nomadism' in medieval Europe were by no means ethnically or socially homogenous. At a very general level it is possible to divide the nomadic population of late medieval Europe into two main groups. In the Mediterranean world, Gypsies and Romanies were largely sedentary and had well-developed social networks which allowed a considerable degree of social interchange with settled society and with other nomadic groups. In northern and western Europe, Gypsies and Travellers were, and still are, largely nomadic. The Traveller population of contemporary Europe includes the Manouche in France, Belgium and Holland; the Sinti and Jenisch of Germany and German-speaking countries; the Mercheros of Spain, and the Reisende and Taterne of Norway.[21] Estimates of Europe's nomadic population vary enormously. They range from a low of two million to a high of five million.[22] By no means are all of these nomadic. Liegeois has estimated the nomadic element at twenty-five per cent of the total 'travelling' population in the European Union. An estimated thirty per cent are partially nomadic and almost forty per cent are sedentary or only irregularly nomadic.[23] A recent study by Hickland shows that Traveller mobility within Ireland varies significantly from one community, and one region, to another. Also, unlike 'settled people' who possess what C. Wright Mills calls the 'sociological imagination', Travellers, or at least the nomadic element of the population, have what Harvey calls a highly developed 'geographical imagination'.[24] They think across space and place and regard geographical mobility as an integral, but by no means defining, feature of their way of life. Hickland shows that Tuam Travellers are more 'settled' than those in Cork city, many of whom move around within Munster. She writes:

> The Tuam population who do travel do so without moving their entire household. They travel by bus or train for a fixed and limited period of time. For Cork Travellers, however, movement is an integral part of their existence. Their mobility is highly seasonal, with most movement occurring during the summer months and corresponding with annual fairs and festivals which take place primarily at this time.[25]

Gypsies still roam freely throughout northern India which is the cradle of the Romany people, particularly in the desert state of Rajasthan. Table 1 shows their present distribution in Europe and in former Soviet satellites. It is clear from this table that Europe's Travelling peoples are especially concentrated in eastern Europe and the former Soviet Union. In Romania, the seventeen Gypsy tribes make up thirteen per cent of the total population. As eastern European countries adopt free-market policies and follow a Western route to capitalist development, it is highly probable that they will also inherit the West's anti-Traveller racism. The social distance between the settled population and nomadic communities will increase, thus giving rise to further anti-Gypsy racism. Even today, the modernisation and transformation of post-Soviet satellites is leading to economic insecurity among eastern Europe's Gypsy and Romany populations. This is causing an eastward drift of nomadic communities, especially to Germany, which initially accommodated Gypsies to make amends for Nazi killings. Recently, however, it has been sending thousands of Gypsies and Travellers back to Romania and other eastern European countries to placate the utlra-right and neo-fascist elements. The rise of anti-Gypsy prejudice throughout Europe means that nomadic communities find it increasingly difficult to cross political borders.

This is not only true of Gypsies in Portugal, Spain and France. It is also a problem experienced by Irish Travellers, many of whom were forced out of London and southern England as a result of a rise in anti-Traveller feeling and economic insecurity during the Thatcher years. We have also recently seen flare-ups of anti-Traveller prejudice in this country, especially at Christmas and during the holiday season when Irish Travellers working in England return home for weddings, funerals or seasonal gatherings. Local farmers and businesses point to the inconvenience that this causes the settled community. Travellers for their part argue that, given the lack of suitable halting sites, they have no other choice but to park wherever they can on such occasions.

Eoin MacNeill suggests that Irish Travellers are descendants of the pre-Christian semonrige or 'rivet-makers' who were a privileged minority caste in pre-Gaelic Ireland, but were subsequently demoted to inferior positions by invading Gaels.[26] The first mention of Travellers in Ireland refers to whitesmiths in the fifth century. This artisanate 'travelled the Irish countryside making personal ornaments, weapons and horsetrappings in exchange for food and lodging'.[27] As elsewhere in Europe, Travellers in pre-colonial Ireland were usually associated with certain occupations. In the late colonial period they still performed important social functions, not least by linking together scattered and mutually suspicious communities and transmitting information from one part of the country to another. In periods of political and social unrest they may indeed have flourished through the use of the secrecy that suspicion encouraged. They were also often victimised as 'outsiders' and 'spies' by 'settlers' and the settled population alike. Certainly, 'tinkers', pedlars and vagrants were discriminated against in colonial Ireland. They were regularly penalised by the monarchy, both in England and in early colonial Ireland, from the sixteenth century onwards. Thus King Edward VI passed an 'Acte for tynkers and pedlars' in 1552 which stipulated that:

> . . . no person or persons called tynker, pedlar, or pety chapman shall wander or go from one towne to another or form place to place out of the towne, parish or village.[28]

Acton shows how the Tudor period witnessed a massive shakeout of agricultural labour which contributed to the nomadisation of large sections of rural society. These provided the human resources for the growth of a mercantile economy. He also shows how the 'sturdy beggars' and the 'vagrants' of Elizabethan England became the 'hate objects' of the establishment that 'welfare-spongers' are today. They were blamed without qualification for their own fate. Then, as now, this gave rise to a general phenomenon of national, ethnic and religious xenophobic scapegoating which targeted Travellers in particular.[29] Professional Travellers in sixteenth- and seventeenth-century Ireland were often skilled craftsmen and men of special gifts. These included poets, genealogists, seers, druids, doctors and historians, as well as skilled craftsmen, many of whom may have been considered an inferior category in the general 'travelling' population. Many of these were compelled to travel because of the small size and separatist nature of the tribal society. Moreover, the subsistence nature of the tribal economy in Ireland meant that clans could not support a full complement of professionals whose services were only needed intermittently. This encouraged the growth of a travelling artisanate. In a country where towns were literally few and far between, and where political centralisation was weak, Travellers were often the only national institution and they provided the social cement which bound isolated communities together. Thus, whereas tribal integrity was embodied in the person of the chief or 'taoiseach', inter-tribal continuity was embodied in the professional Travellers.[30]

Ní Shuinear identifies three strands in the origins debate relating to Travellers in Ireland. The first insists that Travellers are drop-outs from 'normal society', victims of their own inadequacy

– a relatively new phenomenon dating from the Famine, or at most from the Cromwellian era.[31] As she shows, one strand of this argument is closely associated with the culture of poverty debate which holds that Traveller society is riddled with alcoholism, chronic unemployment and criminality and that this indicates that Travellers or 'tinkers' are the descendants of problem-ridden persons who had to drop out of society because they were unable to cope with it. An extreme variant of this view was recently propounded by Helen Lucy Burke. She insisted that Traveller culture was inferior to that of the settled population and went on to argue that 'itinerant culture' does not stand up to scrutiny. According to her it was a culture where women were 'treated like pack animals' and was characterised by large families and 'child marriage contributing to ill health and frequent deaths'.[32] This view treats Traveller 'culture' as pathologically responsible for all Traveller problems and holds that Travellers are social misfits, descendants of social deviants whose deviance is pathological and incurable. Travellers, for that very reason, should not be allowed to settle near 'settled' communities. This perspective also seriously devalues Traveller culture and portrays Travellers as an unassimilable and 'unmeltable' minority. A second strand in the origins debate suggests that Travellers are the relics of a pre-Celtic group relegated to inferior positions by Celtic invaders from the fifth century onwards. This view at least encourages comparisons between Travellers, Gypsies, 'outcasts' and 'untouchables' in other countries including India, Spain, Italy and Romania. It also avoids the pitfalls of 'ethnic exceptionalism' which emphasises the ethnic distinctiveness, and neglects the socio-economic similarities between different Travellers and Gypsy communities throughout Europe.

The third strand in the origins debate identifies Irish Travellers as descendants of indigenous nomadic craftsmen who never acquired property or settled down. Ní Shuinear suggests that highly-crafted ironwork, jewellery, weapons and tools of the Celtic period could

Table 1: Distribution of nomadic people in contemporary Europe.*

Finland	70,000
Scandinavia	17,000
Austria	20,000
Ireland	22,000
Switzerland	30,000
Poland	40,000
Benelux	45,000
Albania	90,000
Great Britain	90,000
Italy	90,000
Germany	110,000
Greece	160,000
France	280,000
Turkey	300,000
Former USSR	306,000
Hungary	550,000
Spain	650,000
Former Yugoslavia	698,000
Bulgaria	700,000
Czech/Slovak Republics	730,000
Romania	1,800,000

* Figures are EU minimum estimates. *Source:* Focus, 1994.

never have been crafted by peasants but must instead have been the work of highly-skilled and specialised craftworkers. As quasi-nomadic, pastoral communities in Celtic Ireland gradually became more sedentary with people living in dispersed, low-density settlements throughout the country, Travellers existed to service this surplus-producing society. They traded agricultural surpluses for finely-crafted metalwork and other ornate craftwork. Mc Veigh suggests that the original Irish nomadic population may also have been supplemented at various times in Irish history by dispossessed labourers and other marginalised people. Gradually this population 'developed a clear sense of its distinct social and cultural identity which was bounded by overt prejudice and racism from the sedentary Irish community'.[33] This anti-Traveller racism, as we shall see, was constructed on the anvil of a deepening 'sedentarism'. It was also forged upon the proprietorial sense of pride, and sense of place, of an emergent nationalist bourgeoisie and tenant farmer class throughout the late nineteenth and early twentieth centuries. It is maintained today by the practice of defending the dominant ethnicity at all costs and according it all political and economic power. The following section traces the origins of this racialisation of Travellers to Enlightenment thinking, the growth of nationalism and the emergence of stageist theories of development which have relegated nomadic peoples to the lowest rungs of the social hierarchy.

2. Capitalism, Nationalism and the Racialisation of Nomads and Travellers

The prestigious position of Travellers in Gaelic Ireland contrasts sharply with their 'outcastness' in nationalist Ireland and their radical exclusion from contemporary Irish society. This in turn led to them being associated with animalism, uncleanliness and criminality. However, anti-Traveller and 'anti-nomad' sentiment was not a peculiarity of the Irish. Beginning with the Enlightenment, European philosophy, and later on the social sciences, prioritised sedentarism over nomadism and literally denigrated nomadism by portraying it as a characteristic of 'barbarous' people. The racialisation of Europe's large Traveller and Gypsy communities reached unprecedented heights during the Darwinian nation-building period of the nineteenth century. Indeed, the fusion of social Darwinism with bourgeois nationalism during this time contributed to a radical disavowal of Gypsy and Traveller claims for special treatment. As we have already seen, the denigration of Travellers and Gypsies has long been a feature of European political discourse. It was particularly central to general evolutionary theories of development which prioritised the rights of the individual over those of the community. It was also evident in theories which defended bourgeois property rights, which legitimised the domination of nomadic societies in the colonies by white 'settlers' and which justified the marginalisation of nomadic groups including Gypsies, Travellers and the rural poor within Europe, on the grounds that, as propertyless people, they had no right to be included within the political or moral structures of European societies.

Hugo Grotius was among the first to suggest that the development of laws, culture and civilisation was intimately linked to the evolution of man-land relations over time and space. Quoting sacred history, he suggested that primitive common ownership of movable objects and immovable property was abandoned because 'men were not content to feed on the spontaneous products of the earth, to dwell in caves, to have the body either naked or clothed in the bark of trees or skins of wild animals, but chose a more refined mode of life; this gave rise to industry'.[34] John Locke also contributed to the prioritisation of propertied interests and the marginalisation of the propertyless when he suggested that primitive societies approached enlightenment by abandoning communal ownership of goods and services, by respecting private property and by espousing individual rights over the rights of communities.[35] Moreover, unlike many of his predecessors Locke did not trace the origin of private property to any social 'pact'. He linked it instead to the abandonment of 'primitive' lifestyles associated with the 'travelling life' and nomadism. He further suggested that private property arose when men mixed their labour with resources drawn from the material world. This not only meant that the more people invested labour in the material world, the more they legitimised its privatisation, it also meant that Travellers and Gypsies, who made no claims on property and did not 'accumulate' wealth, had neither political nor social rights in state-centred capitalist societies. Like most Enlightenment philosophers, Locke regarded primitive peoples, including Europe's nomadic and Travelling peoples, as lacking the essential characteristics of civilisation – statehood, urban centres, literature and art. Indeed he suggested that, where they were not wards of Enlightened rulers, Gypsies, Travellers and the propertyless poor were a threat to European civilization itself.

Similarly, Adam Smith, one of the earliest exponents of a stageist approach to social progress, used resource utilisation as a basis for classifying societies and for arranging them in a hierarchical order. Travellers and Gypsies in Europe, and nomadic societies in the colonies, occupied the lowest rungs of the social hierarchy.[36] Writing in the 1760s, Semyon Desnitsky, a Russian student of Smith, outlined four distinctive stages in the evolution of civilised societies. Starting with 'primordial' societies of 'noble savages', he argued that nomadism was the most primitive stage of development because it was 'the condition of people living by hunting animals and feeding on the spontaneous fruits of the earth'. The second stage was 'the condition of people living as shepherds, or the pastoral [stage]'. The third stage was that attained by sedentary agriculturalists. The fourth and highest stage of development was attained by societies engaged in commerce, specifically in long-distance and international trade.

Like all stageist theories of development, those of Grotius, Locke and Smith were based on the premise that each stage in the evolution of society was characterised by a different mode of subsistence, rather than simply by different forms of social and political organisation. What is important to note here, however, is that their writings contributed to the racialisation of nomadic culture which later on gave pseudo-scientific sanction to the general marginalisation of Traveller communities and Gypsies in nineteenth-century nationalist ideologies. Irish attitudes towards 'tinkers' and Travellers in the nineteenth century were certainly influenced by social Darwinism. They were also influenced by evolutionary theory in general and by the growth of bourgeois nationalist ideals. The fusion of these with the territorial imperative of nation-builders had clear implications for Travellers and other minority groups in nineteenth-century Ireland. Once again, however, this was not a peculiarity of the Irish. It was characteristic of nationalisms throughout Europe and North America where, as a result of the rise of the bourgeois nation-state with its intricate administrative and surveillance systems, Travellers and Gypsies had less and less room for manoeuvre. This was particularly clear in the writings of Friedrich Ratzel, the German political geographer, who did so much to justify the coercive domination of native peoples in the colonial world and the containment of subordinate social groups within Europe. For Ratzel:

> . . . the struggle for existence means a struggle for space . . . A superior people, invading the territory of its weaker savage neighbours, robs them of their land, forces them back into corners too small for their support, and continues to encroach even upon this meagre possession, till the weaker finally loses the last remnants of its domain, is literally crowded off the earth . . . The superiority of such expansionists consists primarily in their greater ability to appropriate, thoroughly utilize and populate territory'.[37]

Given the racist character of Ratzel's theorising, especially his racialisation of pre-capitalist communities like Gypsies, Romanies and other Travellers, it is not surprising that his writings were later used to provide the intellectual basis of Nazi policies justifying the extermination of Gypsies in Europe. Indeed Ratzel devised a profoundly ethnocentric theory of social progress which ranked sedentarism and the nation-state above nomadic societies. Writing in a period which saw the Western bourgeoisie appropriating more and more of the earth's surface, he also suggested that this was a perfectly natural development which could be explained in terms of evolutionary theory. Arguing from deep nationalist convictions, he further claimed that sedentary peoples, particularly those in the more powerful nation-states of Europe, had first claim on the world's resources because their approach to environmental management was superior to the environmental practices of nomadic peoples and pre-capitalist societies. Like other evolutionary theories, Ratzel's ideas were refracted through social class and ethnic lenses in such a way as to suggest that there was literally no room for Travellers and Gypsies in nation-building Europe. As Gypsies and 'tinkers', they were social anachronisms, a 'dirty people' who were not entitled to participation in, or protection from, the dominant institutions which constituted the material and moral structures of bourgeois Europe. This type of anti-Traveller and anti-nomad racism was deeply rooted in an ideology of sedentarist superiority which regarded 'unsettled' people as racially inferior to settled people. So convincing were these ideas that they still unconsciously influence the way we think about Travellers in contemporary Ireland and the way we regard Gypsies and Romanies in contemporary Europe.

The consolidation of nations and the growth of nationalism certainly aggravated anti-Traveller and anti-Gypsy prejudice in Europe throughout the nineteenth century. It also contributed to the racialisation of these groups well into the twentieth century. Nowhere was this more noticeable than in Ireland where, as L.P. Curtis has noted, popular histories contrasted Saxon and Celt in such a way as to elevate the former over the latter on the grounds that their deep attachment to the land where they lived rendered Anglo-Saxons superior to the more nomadic Celts. The Celts in turn were simianised because they were descended from nomadic peoples and as such were socially inferior to Anglo-Saxons. Thus Curtis argues that:

> The politically mature and emotionally stable, virile and enlightened Saxon yeoman emerged as the heroic archetype immeasurably superior in all respects to the clannish, primitive, excitable and feminine Celt'.[38]

Curtis went on to suggest that the racial and emotional antithesis between Anglo-Saxon and Celt contained many reassuring features for respectable Victorians who were apprehensive about the ability of the Anglo-Saxon race to flourish and about the capacity of their own class to survive the growing menace of democratisation, social mobility and alien or Celtic immigration which was considered as a nineteenth-century variant of nomadism.[39]

Thus nineteenth-century Irish attitudes towards themselves, and towards 'tinkers' and Travellers in their midst, must be analysed against the background of a European tradition which prioritised sedentarism over nomadism and which legitimised the social and cultural values of settled communities and property-owners while undermining the position of the propertyless. In this tradition, nationalism, together with the cultural and territorial imperatives of nation-builders, was equated with progress and growth. Nomadism on the other hand, and Travelling communities within Ireland, were looked on as social anomalies, relics from a 'barbarous' past that was best forgotten because they represented all that was backward, unstable and evil about Irish society.

Also in Ireland and in other post-colonial societies, the construction of national identities aggravated divisions between hegemonic bourgeois culture and counter-hegemonic groups like Travellers and the landless poor. David Lloyd has argued that Ireland conformed to the model of bourgeois nationalism that Franz Fanon analysed in his *Wretched of the Earth*. He also suggests that:

> The adoption, virtually wholesale, of the state institutions of the colonising power, and conformity to its models of representative democracy, poses what Fanon terms the 'sterile formalism' of bourgeois politics against the popular movements its institutions are designed to contain. The state, which represents the point of intersection of the nation with the unilaterally defined universality of the world economic order, becomes a brake on the decolonising process culturally as well as economically.[40]

The construction of an Irish national identity intensified the divide between hegemonic groups like the rural and urban bourgeoisie on the one hand, and the rural poor and urban working class on the other. In more extreme instances this contributed to the racialisation of 'tinkers' or Travellers and the portrayal of the rural poor as the racial inferiors of the hegemonic bourgeoisie.

In constructing nationalist Ireland, the links between modern-day Irish people and early aristocratic Celtic society were also unearthed by historians, playwrights, poets, antiquarians and ethnographers. However, because the lineage of Irish Travellers or 'tinkers' could not be taken for granted in late nineteenth-century Ireland, and not least because their cultural integrity could not be reconstructed in the modern nation, little effort was expended in the defence of the rights of Travellers in nation-building Ireland. Their 'will to travel', and their 'propensity to homelessness' were instead used to hide the very presence of 'tinkers' in an increasingly bourgeois society which struggled for international recognition in an age when these were the attributes of 'inferior peoples'. This had the effect of 'benumbing' Irish sensitivity to the historical value of Traveller culture.[41] It also contributed to the pejorativisation of 'tinkers' who were portrayed as an unmanageable and 'unmeltable' minority in Irish society.[42]

Despite this, 'tinkerism' has embodied many of the dynamics of an ancient, albeit benighted, sense of Irishness in nineteenth- and early twentieth-century Ireland. Court suggests that the contemplation of this 'tinkerism':

> . . . yields a glimpse of the buds that blossomed into several of the most seductive and thorny concepts of the present day: racism, professionalism, commercialism, mass communications, and the species of individualism that compensates for and yet serves the power of the impersonal state.[43]

It also reflects the shortcoming of a bourgeois nationalist ideology of liberation which did not constitute a liberating force for all sectors of Irish society. Travellers were not just excluded from the national agenda. As social outcasts from 'respectable society' they were an ugly blemish on the face of Mother Ireland and were disparaged as a backward people who were to 'settle down' and become wards of the state if they were not to become a threat to the settled social order.

In Ireland, as elsewhere in Europe, nationalism stressed the organic links between 'the people' or 'volk' and their homeland or 'heimat'. The very idea of 'volk' conjured up images of a people linked to the nation through 'blood and soil' and ties of property. Nationalists suggested that the link between the 'volk' and their 'heimat' was an entirely 'natural', quasi-sacred one.[44] However, from the start, the categories 'volk' and 'the people' were exclusionist terms and nationalism, as in Irish nationalism, did not serve this important anchoring or 'territorialising' function for the rural poor (including Travellers, the poorest of the Irish poor) that it did for the better-off. Instead large numbers of them were 'excommunicated' from Ireland through emigration, and groups like Travellers and other minorities were expected to abandon their identity and assimilate into Irish society. As in the late nineteenth century, so also in the post-independence period, the state was silent on the disappearance of the rural poor, especially the travelling poor. It was widely recognized that the new Ireland was to be built not only *by*, but also *for* the 'stalwart, muscular, dauntless young braves' of rural Ireland. Unlike the poor rural communities serviced by Travellers and 'tinkers', these were 'royally endowed with every attribute that goes to make up a peerless and magnificent manhood'.[45] Their disappearance through emigration was to be prevented at all costs because it would deprive Ireland of the very 'bone and sinew' needed for the construction of a healthy nation. The rural poor, not least the 'sad, weeping and melancholy emigrants' from the west of Ireland who had cast off all allegiance to the land, deserved to emigrate. They did not carry with them 'one single reminder of their nationality' when they left the country. 'Tinkers', many of whom lacked the safety-valve of emigration, were deemed inferior to the poorest of the rural poor and were looked upon as a people without land and without history. As such they were considered to have no place in nationalist Ireland.

Thus the roots of anti-Traveller racism are deeply embedded in the social fabric and agrarian structure of nineteenth-century Ireland.

They are also to be found in a post-Famine 'common sense' social Darwinism which insisted that only the strongest should inherit the earth. The meek, ironically, would come into their inheritance in a post-earthly existence. This genre of anti-Traveller and 'anti-tinker' racism is also traceable to a late nineteenth- and early twentieth-century rural fundamentalism which prioritised the values of property-owners over and above those of the propertyless. J.M. Synge, one of the few Irish writers to stand out against this trend, sympathised with 'tramps', 'vagrants' and 'tinkers' both because they represented the marginalised 'other' in an increasingly petty bourgeois society, and because they rejected the mores of that society and were deeply scornful of its shallow, sanitised respectability. In plays like *The Tinker's Wedding* and *The Playboy of the Western World*, 'tinkers' and Travellers inhabit a world apart from that of substantial Catholic tenant farmers. Theirs was a world that was more spontaneous and anarchic, and consequently more authentic, than that which the petty rural bourgeoisie were seeking to construct. In his essay 'The Vagrants of County Wicklow,' Synge rescues 'tramps' and 'tinkers' from cultural oblivion and gives them a place alongside islanders, peasants, potato 'hokers' and fishermen, the neglected and rejected in the bourgeois nationalist pantheon.[46] Synge idealised these sectors of Irish society because they were the social antidotes to a stultifying, puritanical and late-Victorian nationalism that was in danger of suffocating cultural life in early twentieth-century Ireland. As Terry Eagleton has argued in his *Heathcliff and the Great Hunger*, Synge was in many respects a mirror of the society that he inhabited.[47] He was drawn from a beleaguered Anglo-Irish ascendancy and drawn to the folk customs and social life of the rural poor and island communities. He was also rooted in Irish traditionalism and steeped in modern European culture. However, he did not occupy a neutral ground between the two polarities of tradition and modernity, preferring instead to defend the former, particularly the nomadic tradition of 'tinkers' and the spontaneity of the peasantry, from the centralising grasp of the modern nation-state. Moreover, unlike most cultural nationalists and the Catholic Church who were similarly engaged in a prioritisation of the rural over the urban, Synge defended nomadism and the peasantry for their own sake and because they were the wellsprings of naturalism and authenticity. He did not do so in order to consolidate a cultural national hegemony or to advance the political agenda of dominant social classes. Instead, in *The Tinker's Wedding*, he has a Catholic priest – representing the state and respectability – beaten up, thrown into a sack and kidnapped by mischievous 'tinkers' resentful of the ways of 'settled' Ireland. Long before the furore over the staging of *The Playboy of the Western World*, this play was turned down by the Abbey as unsuitable for Dublin audiences.[48] Synge defended the play precisely because it did not fit with the conventional wisdom of the nationalist literati, just as he defended 'tramps' and 'tinkers' because they did not fit into the mould of a conservative Catholic nation-state. Moreover, like the 'Anarchist Prince' Pieter Kropotkin who defended the autonomy of peasant communities and the artisanate from the centralising thrust of the Russian state, Synge elevated the spontaneity and anarchism of 'tinkers' and peasants over a post-Victorian respectability and the stateist objectives of the Catholic bourgeoisie.[49] As Eagelton suggests:

> His focus on the lone character breaking loose from a coercive society is a familiar modernist motif, but the figure around whom it turns is usually the traditional one of the vagrant. It is in the beggar, the outcast, the social misfit that the Anglo-Irish artist can find an objective correlate of his own solitary nonconformism, rather than in some more collective political revolt.[50]

Indeed Synge's peasants and 'tinkers' are natural aristocrats. They upset the artificial bourgeois opposition between Nature and Art, not least by forging a highly artistic and intricate language which comes from the mouths of the people, and talks wondrously of the natural world. They are the 'others' in an increasingly materialistic and settled society, a people whose community life is ample compensation for the barrenness of their material world. Synge did not just 'go native' by fixing a limelight on 'tramps' and 'tinkers' and focusing on the plebeian underside of Irish society. He played the greatest respect to 'tinkers' and vagrants, and paid homage to the lowest rungs of that society, to people whom many considered dispensable in the new Ireland. Fintan O'Toole has suggested that, in identifying with the Aran fisherfolk, Synge the urbanite and the intellectual was perfectly aware of the ironies of the Abbey's cultural nationalist project.[51] Unlike most of his artistic peers, however, his plays were not just about the right of Ireland to decide how it should be represented. They literally sought to establish a space in the theatre so that those outside the mainstream of Irish society would have room to articulate their views on the sanitised new Ireland that was then in the making.

There is a marked contrast between the idealisation and sympathetic treatment of 'tinkers' and vagrants in Synge's writing and their outright neglect and pejorativisation in most contemporary Irish literature. In J.B. Keane's play *The Field*, for example, Travellers are treated as social flotsam and as social degenerates because they have neither roots in, nor respect for, the land.[52] Unlike in Merimee's *Carmen*, for example, where the Gypsy woman is an earthy and sexually attractive exotic 'other' who flaunts her sexuality by flirting with bourgeois society, Keane paints the 'tinker' woman in far darker colours. Like Van Gogh, who literally painted Belgian peasants in colours so dark that they were indistinguishable from the soil they worked and the potatoes they ate, Keane portrays 'tinkers' and 'knackers' in 'earthy' colours. Unlike Van Gogh, however, he does so out of a deep dislike for the poorest of the rural poor, and not out of sympathy for their plight. Thus in *The Field*, the 'tinker woman' is at once a 'dirty tinker' and a 'dirty whore'. In Jim Sheridan's film adaptation of the play she is a red-haired girl who uses her alluring sexuality to entice Bull Mac Cabe's only son off the land. In so doing she encourages him to reject the mores of the landed tenantry and the petty bourgeoisie and to spend his life on the road rather than submitting to patriarchal authority on the farm. Her success would represent a triumph of love and sexuality over love of the land. For that reason the 'tinker woman' was an affront to all patriarchal values because she was literally causing the seed of the patriarch to fall by the wayside, rather than allowing it to take root on the land. The very survival of the Travelling way of life and the profligacy of peasants were widely considered as affronts to the hegemonic ideals of the petty bourgeoisie with their emphasis on hard work and property-ownership as the proper ideals by which honest Irishmen were to live, and which proper Irish women were obliged to respect.

Thus, throughout the late nineteenth and early twentieth centuries there was a marked overlapping between anti-Traveller racism and nationalism in Ireland which goes back to the circumstances in which the Irish nation was conceived as a cradle for bourgeois and petty bourgeois respectability. On the one hand, Irish nationalism, simply considered as a struggle for the control of territory, has striven to control population and to produce an Irish 'people' as a political community.[53] On the other hand, the Irish nation was forged as a historical system of exclusions and dominations. It became a place where the patriarchal values of the rural bourgeoisie occupied pride of place, a place where Irish women were accorded positions as second-class citizens, a place where the child in the womb had rights over and above its mother, a place, finally, where Travellers were scarcely even considered as citizens and were viewed instead as wards of the state. The isolation of Travellers and the fragmentation of their world reduced Travellers to the status of social 'outcasts' in Irish society. This has been reflected in the status of Traveller issues in Irish political discourse. The very terms that we use in addressing Traveller issues effectively closes them out of respectable political discourse. Use of terms like 'knackers' and 'itinerants' debases

Travellers to the level of a racial minority. Their debasement is particularly obvious in the political arena where the very idea of Travellers' rights and of a Traveller vote are anathema to the majority of local and national politicians. The section that follows looks at the rediscovery and reinvention of Travellers in recent years. It also shows how Travellers have been expected to incorporate into Irish society despite widespread opposition.

The neglect and 'rediscovery' of Travellers in post-independence Ireland

Court suggests that Ireland arrived in the middle of the twentieth century as an oddity among the small nations of western Europe:

> Its geography and ethnic attributes had given it certain political and cultural originality, much of which had been paradoxically preserved by four centuries of alien colonisation . . . . The Irish who had preserved and shaped these traditions by active use had also been shaped by them, thus they were not quite like most of their European contemporaries. And even among these countrymen the Tinkers were conspicuous for remaining doggedly true to themselves. In the 1950s and 1960s while the rest of the citizenry strove to shed its local peculiarities and by industrial, financial, and educational development to prepare itself for membership in the 'global village', the Tinkers still pursued the idiosyncratic, mobile style of life that had been indispensable – although in ways a prescribed – element of traditional Irish society.[54]

Through their association with poverty, violence and hardship, it still proved difficult to accommodate 'tinkers' within the dominant institutions of post-independence Ireland. At best they could be assimilated into settled society on that society's terms. At worst their way of life was criminalised. Travellers were victims of social and structural change in a progressively sterile and sanitised society that had less and less need for the services of 'tinkers'. By the 1960s the Irish:

> . . . were not concerned with discovering and evaluating varieties of domestic culture – they instead 'wished to expunge Tinkerism, not to vindicate or assess its significance'.[55]

Irish Travellers were also rediscovered by anthropologists, chiefly American and British, and by ethnographers and folklorists in the post-War period. The adoption of the term 'itinerant' to describe 'tinkers' and Travellers similarly suggested a devaluation of the latter. It signified a wish on the part of mainstream society to 'enrol the Tinkers, undifferentiated, among the nation's labouring poor'. Court suggests that this renaming betokened 'a humane desire to divest Tinker clans of their immemorial outcastness'. It also meant that:

> . . . if Tinkers were to be distinguished from other impoverished Irish *only by superficial characteristics*, then their immense difficulty in assimilating settled values – the difficulty that had given rise to the Report – seemed inexplicable except as wrongheadedness, ignorance, or mere perversity'.[56]

From the 1960s onwards, Travellers suffered the same fate as the far more substantial craftworkers did in the nineteenth century. They found that their crafts and services were increasingly redundant in a progressively 'sanitised' and 'sterilised' society, and in a country where the supermarket had replaced the country markets and fairs that were the mainstays of the informal economy of Travelling people. In moving to cities like Dublin, Cork and Limerick, Travellers became stark reminders of all that urban Ireland wanted to forget. Declan Kiberd has argued that bouts of 'communal amnesia' are characteristic of most post-colonial states, including Ireland in the 1960s.[57] As Neitzche suggests, amnesiacs generally have good strategic reasons for their forgetfulness. From the 1960s onwards, political leaders in modern Ireland, fixated on the project of rural and industrial modernisation, suggested that it was time to 'forget' Ireland's colonial past, and to forget those who did not fit into their image of a progressive modern European state. Well before Fukuyama, they advocated an 'end to history', especially histories of the Famine period, of rebellion and of the rural poor. Nowhere was this more noticeable than in the neglect of Traveller culture and the specific needs of Travelling people by 'official Ireland'. The Irish Folklore Commission, established in 1935 to document and preserve Irish oral traditions, made little effort to survey or record the lives of travelling people. Court suggests that this 'oversight' seemed especially untoward given that the Commission was:

> . . . one of the most effective such agencies in western Europe, renowned for its well-organised, intensive study of many spheres of national life. As much as it represented careful husbanding of national resources, the institutional lack of interest in Tinkers was a political decision.[58]

To the extent that Irish Travellers were perceived as having any history, theirs was not a history in any cumulative or purposeful sense. It was instead an endless and monotonous cycle of hardship and poverty. The folk culture, social rituals and religious superstitions that were central to the survival of Travelling people were incomprehensible to the official Irish mind. Like the peasantry of southern

Italy described by Carlo Levi in the 1930s, Irish Travellers in post-independence Ireland were assumed to have not so much a history as a mythology. They existed outside the framework of Irish historical time and were confined instead to 'that which is changeless and eternal'.[59] Like Levi's Italian peasantry, Ireland's Travellers were forced to resign themselves to being dominated. They did not feel as their own the glories and undertakings of a bourgeois and petty bourgeois Ireland which was increasingly their enemy. Like the Mexican Indian peasantry in Traven's novel *Government*, Irish Travellers also were a people 'without a country to belong to, without the right to call themselves members [of the nation]', a people 'riven hither and thither by every pull of the wind'.[60]

Despite their pejorativisation, however, Irish Travellers, like Gypsies elsewhere in Europe, sustained their externally well-defined 'subculture' in the changing circumstances of twentieth-century Irish society. Although they found themselves from time to time the focus of settled politics, they declined, until recently, to organise themselves to long-term political purpose. Neither, until recently, did they take any interest in, or show any allegiance to, settled political processes. As in other European nations, Travellers' interests in Ireland were deemed an intellectual diversion. Their problems were judged a social annoyance, their history was considered an anomaly and their very presence was considered inessential at best, and, at worst, a threat to the well-being and interests of settled society.[61] The following chapter discusses the changing geography and sociology of Travelling communities since the 1960s and the new politics of exclusion which are literally pushing Travellers to the margins of Irish society.

3. The Transformation of Traveller Society, 1960–1995

In the early 1960s it was estimated that there were 3,167 Travellers over the age of 14 years in Ireland. Of the 769 who claimed to be economically active, 600 were tin-smiths, 103 were chimney sweeps and 36 were flower makers.[62] Others had employment as seasonal workers, including farm labourers, and most of these lived in conditions of extreme poverty which accelerated their drift to urban areas. Travellers then were still attached to a disintegrating, traditional world, one that was going to change very dramatically with the onset of the Lemass years and with entry into the European Community. Urban Travellers even then, however, were already taking to scrap-dealing, including car-dismantling, and, in the Sixties, these jobs provided a lucrative income for some Traveller families at least. A number of other Travellers became successful traders. But what transformed the income position of the Travellers in the 1960s most of all was the availability of unemployment assistance. This meant that the conditions of extreme economic poverty that formerly prevailed among many rural Traveller communities were all but wiped out with the rise of the welfare state. Nevertheless, as Table 2 indicates, the living conditions of Travellers in the early Sixties left a lot to be desired. As the travelling community faced urban living, they still retained much of the baggage they inherited from literally living on the roadside. This is particularly noticeable in the case of the large numbers of Travellers living in tents and horse-drawn caravans. In December 1960, just under thirty per cent of Traveller families were living in roadside tents. Less than five per cent of them were housed. The majority of Travellers were still living in traditional horsedrawn caravans and a very small number

Table 2: Traveller accommodation in Ireland, 1960.

Type of Accommodation	No. of Families	Percentage Total
House	43	3.6
Room	13	1.1
Horsedrawn caravan	674	56.3
Horsedrawn caravan/tent	64	5.3
Trailer caravan	60	5.1
Tent	335	28.0
No accommodation	9	0.6
Total	1198	100

Source: Appendix XXXII, *Report of the Commission on Itinerancy*, 1963.

indeed owned modern trailer caravans.[63] In the early Sixties, it was also recognised that, while Travellers shared a common ethnicity, Traveller society was beginning to be stratified in terms of occupation and status. At that time, the pyramid of Traveller society was occupied by some 60–70 families engaged in scrap-dealing and, to a lesser extent, horse-trading, and more and more families were moving into the antique trade and furniture business. Although at first glance the families were comparatively well-off, their wealth was extremely 'fluid' and they rarely had possession of it at any one time. As Barnes has pointed out, it was often instead 'on loan' among Traveller families lower down the social hierarchy.[64] This group generally ranged far and wide throughout the country, often moving freely between Ireland and England, and to a lesser extent than before, Scotland.

Below this 'Traveller aristocracy' in the 1960s were 200–300 families who were similarly engaged in scrap-dealing and the antique and carpet trade but whose market was far narrower than that of wealthy Travellers. Both these groups managed the transition from tradition to modernity by capitalising upon the modernisation of rural Ireland. They particularly benefited from the 'bungalow blitz' which hit Ireland in the Sixties and Seventies. Travellers belonging to this second group owned trailers which were valued not so much for the status that they conferred but chiefly because they enhanced the economic position of Travellers and made them less dependent upon the welfare state. Below these two groups were approximately 850 families who were among the poorest Travellers in the country. Their geographical range was far narrower and they were far more dependent upon the welfare state than their social superiors. Hickland notes that, despite the disjointed nature of the list of Traveller occupations, there is an underlying commonality in that all working Travellers prefer 'to be self-employed than to be in paid employment and to have flexibility of occupation rather than job security'.[65] She also argues that, although many of the occupations that we associate with Travellers have disappeared in recent decades, the underlying values of Traveller independence and flexibility remain.

Power in Traveller society in the Sixties was usually acquired through the control of lower-class Travellers by a small number of Traveller patriarchs who were prominent in the scrap-dealing business. Thus Barnes has noted, 'the major scrap-dealers often form alliances across traditional lines based on economics rather than social affiliation'.[66] Members of this Traveller élite often act as bankers for poorer Travellers whose economic independence is often completely undermined by control from the top. According to Barnes:

> The rise of scrap-dealers has ensured the insularity of Travellers as a group, yet has widened the gap between rich and poor and has placed the lower-class Travellers into what [Oscar] Lewis has described as the subculture of poverty. This is characterised by complete family disorganisation, low wages, chronic unemployment,

> shortage of cash, absence of savings, lack of property ownership. There is further evidence that patriarchs of families who would have been normally revered for feats of strength, and who relied on ascribed status within the concentric circles of the extended family, have attuned their standards to achieved status demanded by the major scrap-dealers.[67]

The problem with this explanation is that it totally exonerates settled society from any part in the impoverishment of the large number of Travellers occupying the lowest rungs of Traveller society. As John O'Connell of the Dublin Travellers Education and Development Group correctly points out, settled people frequently find an explanation for the distinctiveness of Travellers solely in terms of poverty and deprivation. To the extent that they acknowledge that Travellers have a different way of life, they usually discuss it in terms of a subculture of poverty and suggest that, as a way of life, it would disappear if the problems of Traveller poverty were tackled.[68] Settled people also 'demonise' wealthy Travellers and depict them as patriarchs who are the sole source of other Travellers' problems. In so doing they not only over-estimate the number of wealthy Travellers, they also suggest that as 'traders' they should be taxed and monitored because they are not 'real Travellers' to be housed and cared for by an over-taxed, settled population. This perspective, which has been gaining in popularity since the Seventies, ignores the wider structural and institutional context within which Traveller poverty and powerlessness are generated. In particular, it ignores the mechanisms at work in the wider community within which Travellers are constituted as a disadvantaged and entrapped minority by the settled community.

The total number of persons recorded as Travellers by the Commission on Itinerancy in 1960 was 6,591 or 5.5 per family. The Irish Economic and Social Research Institute recorded a population of 1,396 persons in 224 families with an average of 6.23 persons per family in the Dublin area alone in 1977. The Report of the Travelling People Review Body found that the number of Traveller families in the country as a whole more than doubled from almost 1,200 to just under 2,500 between 1961 and 1980.[69] It increased by almost 50 per cent from 1,690 to 2,490 between 1974 and 1980. Traveller activists today estimate the total Traveller population at just over 22,000. In addition to this, there may be as many as 15,000 Irish Travellers in Britain and a further 10,000 in the United States.[70] We have no accurate estimates of the Irish Traveller population in countries like Germany, France and the Netherlands although evidence suggests that more and more Travellers are travelling in these and other European countries.

Because of the drift towards urban centres within Ireland, the increase in the Traveller population was not uniform either between one county and another or within individual counties. In the Dublin area alone there were 573 families in 1981. This compared with 387 families two years earlier. As the Traveller Review Body indicated, the large number of Travellers in Dublin (compared with a mere handful in the late 1940s and the still very small number in the

Table 3: Growth in number of Traveller families, 1960–1980.

Year	Number of Families	Annual % Increase
1960	1,198	—
1974	1,690	2.5
1975	1,790	5.9
1976	1,874	4.7
1977	1,953	4.2
1978	2,068	5.9
1979	2,293	10.9
1980	2,490	8.6

Source: Appendix III and Appendix IV of the Report of the Commission and the Annual Accounts.

early 1960s) poses an obviously serious problem of accommodation. The Report went on to state that:

> If traveller families were distributed by county in the same proportion as the national population Dublin would, by 1980, have some one-third of the total of 2,490 families i.e. 830. However, the large numbers of families actually in Dublin, compared with a mere handful there in the late 1940s and their still very small number in the early 1960s, poses an obviously serious problem of accommodation. Those who are not in houses, or otherwise accommodated, are concentrated on the outskirts of cities, towns and villages. Generally, they are looked upon as mere trespassers without rights of any sort on road margins and other public land and occasionally on private property. Most of them are likely to be moved on from time to time and some repeatedly.[71]

The pattern of Traveller accommodation had also altered dramatically between 1960 and 1980. This is well borne-out by comparing Table 2 with Table 4. By 1980 just under forty per cent of Travellers were housed. The corresponding figure for 1960 was only four per cent. In 1980 a further fifteen per cent were living on serviced sites. In that year also, however, almost half of all families were still living on the roadside and there were almost three hundred Traveller families on the roadside in the Dublin area alone. The corresponding figures for Limerick, Cork and County Meath, which also recorded high concentrations of poor Travellers, were ninety, eighty-five and eighty families respectively.[72]

The Review Body also found that the average annual increase in the number of families between 1960–1974 was 2.5 per cent. Between 1974–1978 the number of families increased on average

Table 4: Traveller accommodation in Ireland, 1980.

Type of Accommodation	No. of Families	Percent of Total
Living in house	957	38.4
Living on serviced site		
(i) in chalet	253	10.2
(ii) in trailer caravan	131	5.3
Living on roadside	1,149	46.1
Totals	2,490	100

Source: Annual Count for 1980.

by ninety-five per year or five per cent. These are extraordinarily high rates of increase compared with those for the settled population. Among the factors responsible for increase in the Traveller population were early marriage, the rarity of unmarried women of child-bearing age and the high fertility at marriage of Traveller women. However, these factors alone could not possibly account for the total increase in the Traveller population since the Sixties. This must be attributed to a change in the level of emigration among Travellers which was especially heavy in the 1950s and early 1960s and the subsequent return to this country of many families who had emigrated. This occurred particularly during the Thatcher years when hostility towards Irish Travellers in Britain appeared to reach new heights. Indeed, Irish Travellers in Britain face double discrimination both as Travellers and as Irish people. Having no permanent address often exposes them to long delays in receiving benefit payments. Also, as a result of recent reforms of the Caravan's Sites Act (1968) they are often forced off roadside sites into low-standard housing. One recent report suggests that the possible criminalisation of Travellers and the travelling life in contemporary Britain will particularly hit Irish as well as New Travellers by hindering their access to social welfare benefits and

Table 5: Age specific fertility rates (per 1,000 women) for Travellers in Ireland, 1987.

Age	National population	Travellers	Housed	Unhoused
15–19	16.0	78.9	23.7	162.3
20–24	74.9	246.9	131.1	331.7
25–29	146.8	274.7	160.0	386.7
30–34	133.8	250.0	173.5	346.8
35–39	69.1	148.0	94.0	210.9
40–44	20.8	53.1	48.5	62.5
45–49	1.2	11.1	7.9	18.9

Source: Barry, Herity and Solan, 1987.

increasing their racialisation and victimisation by local authority offices.[73] This report also documented an upsurge of anti-Traveller racism in the British press. Irish Travellers in particular are portrayed as though they were pathologically associated with crime and violence, rather than victims of discrimination and poverty. The prejudice of employers, coupled with high rates of illiteracy among adult Travellers, also make British cities highly hostile places for Irish Travellers seeking to escape victimisation and lack of opportunity at home. This means that, like their counterparts in the settled population, they are forced to rely on the welfare state as a safety net for reducing their descent into absolute poverty. It also means that the British press regularly depicts Irish Travellers as 'dole spongers' constantly in search of welfare handouts. Indeed, despite their far smaller numbers, the plight of Irish Travellers in Britain today is not that different from that of pauperised Irish immigrants who were often forced back to Ireland by Poor Law legislation in the first half of the nineteenth century. In terms reminiscent of the anti-Asian and anti-Black racism of the Sixties and Seventies, one English tabloid recently suggested that the only obstacle between large numbers of

Travellers in Ireland and a 'British paradise' was 'the price of a one-way ticket from Dublin to Liverpool into the arms of the British social services'. It went on to argue that 'the residents of the shanty towns studded around Dublin know that the State handouts are bigger, better and easier to come by on the other side of the Irish Sea'.[74] Alongside reports of young 'unskilled and unemployed' Irish people 'flooding' into England to join the dole queue, the English tabloid press regularly carries stories depicting 'Irish tinkers' as 'dirty, ignorant, maladorous, messy and thieving'. Here indeed Ireland is portrayed as a country where local politicians 'vie for popularity by having 'tinkers' shifted before they have a chance to shift any movable property belonging to their constituents and where farmers frequently move them at gunpoint if the police have not already obliged them by using more diplomatic means'. England, on the other hand, is a 'tinker's paradise', 'an attractive proposition', and a place 'where there is more going in the way of casual labour with which tinkers have been known to supplement their income from time to time'.[75]

The increase in the number of Travelling people in Ireland, their location relative to settled communities, and growing concentrations of Travellers in urban centres and agricultural heartlands along the east coast have undoubtedly contributed to an increase in anti-Traveller prejudice in the Seventies and Eighties. In the Fifties and Sixties, the majority of Irish Travellers were rural dwellers. They were dispersed in small encampments throughout the countryside, especially in mixed farming districts in the west of Ireland, and travelled from place to place in small groups of five to six families. They travelled with comparative ease among the settled population of small, mixed farmers and moved from one location to another as their services were needed. With the exception of Dublin, which has long had a sizeable Traveller population, there were very few Traveller families in the eastern counties. The county with the largest concentration in the early Sixties was Galway, which had 142 families in December 1961 and 135 in June, 1962. This increased to 255 families in the early Eighties. The Commission on Itinerancy reported in 1960:

> Apart from those in or near Dublin city the encampments are seldom large and usually consist of groups not exceeding three or four caravans except on special occasions such as Puck Fair, Killorglin, the annual fair at Cahirmee, Galway, and Killarney races, and similar events when large numbers of travellers gathered together.[76]

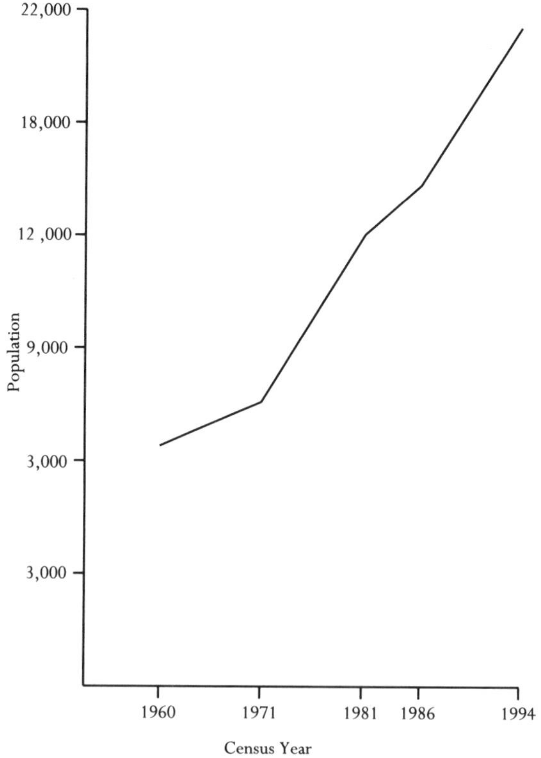

Source: Barry and Daly, 1988

Fig. 1: Traveller population, 1960–1994.

The role that Travellers played at these fairs was highly ambivalent. At the Ballinasloe fair and the Cahirmee horse fair in County Cork, Travellers were either 'hawkers' or managers of certain stalls or booths. They also acted as 'go-betweens' in the bargaining that went on between local buyers and sellers. Their linguistic ability, and especially their skills in 'painting up' horses, gave Travellers a certain amount of status within the rural community. Travellers often got what was called 'boot money' in return for their services at these fairs.[77] The decline of these fairs, and the gentrification and commercialisation of events like the Killarney Races and Puck Fair, meant that events that were formerly open to Travellers were now progressively closed. With farm mechanisation, Travellers also lost out as horse-dealers. As plastic replaced tin throughout the Sixties and Seventies they also lost out as tinsmiths and coppersmiths. As farming itself took on many of the refinements of city life, the distinction between town and country was blurred and a whole range of arts and crafts normally associated with Travellers were now redundant.

The decline of rural fairs has also meant that Travellers no longer have major meeting places where they can profitably congregate. Indeed, by the late Eighties, Traveller families were being moved constantly by local authorities and by the Gardaí. The methods employed to move them have varied from forcible eviction by the local residents to the digging of trenches around Traveller encampments, the erection of earthworks and the dumping of rubbish and used cars around their caravans on a regular basis. Many families are so intimidated by these actions, and by the repeated threats of 'officials' or other residents, that they do not wait for formal eviction but often move themselves to some other patch of wasteland, from which they will yet again be forced to move. The very large numbers of caravans parked on the waste ground, development land and by the roadside are, to say the least, unsightly and damaging to the environment. However,

Table 6: The distribution of Travelling people by selected counties in 1986.

Highest distribution		Lowest distribution	
Dublin	22.0 %	Leitrim	0.7 %
Galway	13.5 %	Cavan	0.9 %
Cork	8.2 %	Carlow	1.0 %
Limerick	7.9 %	Monaghan	1.1 %

Source: Barry and Daly, 1986.

as an *Irish Times* editorial stated, there is 'no point in the settled community complaining about dirt, litter and unsocial behaviour when no effort is made by the authorities to introduce those services generally available to ordinary house-holders'.[78]

The move from rural to urban areas has certainly given rise to large Traveller encampments around Dublin, Limerick, Cork and Galway. Conditions in these camps are equally uncomfortable for Travellers and for the settled population. This is particularly the case in the Clondalkin and Blanchardstown areas where the increase in the Traveller population is causing overcrowding and contributing to anti-Traveller prejudice. These encampments have rather exaggeratedly been compared to the shanty towns that encircled many Latin American cities in the Sixties and Seventies. Whichever way they are viewed, they are breeding grounds for crime against settled communities and for anti-Traveller racism. Thus they have been responsible for a wide range of health and social problems that would not be acceptable in settled society. They also contribute to a build-up of tension and exacerbate the antagonism between the settled community and Travellers. Two recent surveys reported that attitudes of settled people towards Travellers deteriorated significantly between 1972 and 1990, not least in urban areas. There is every indication that they have deteriorated still further since the early Nineties and that they will continue to do so for some time to come. Because Travellers operate within an informal economy where their incomes are untaxed, they will continue to be maligned by disgruntled taxpayers in the settled community. Residents' associations and local farmers frequently also criticise Travellers for 'rubbishing' built-up areas, permitting horses to graze freely in residential areas, allowing dogs free rein in sheep farming districts and blocking country roads with their large seasonal encampments. These criticisms will continue to be made so long as Travellers and settled communities are pitched against each other in the narrow ground available to Irish Travellers today. The only way that they can be resolved is through the breakdown of self-serving stereotypes that set the settled community against Travellers; through improved communication between settled communities and Travellers; through more hard-stand halting sites to accommodate travelling communities, and through more consideration by Travellers of the more legitimate complaints of farmers and local residents. As we shall see below, this is becoming increasingly difficult in an atmosphere where vigilante-type attacks on isolated Traveller communities are on the increase and where anti-Traveller prejudice is literally pushing Travellers to the very edges of Irish society.

Ever since the Seventies, discrimination against Travellers has been systematic. As we have already seen, attacks by anti-Traveller vigilante groups have also been on the increase. By the late Eighties it was widely recognised that feelings of alienation among the Travellers, and the settled population alike, could only lead to anti-social behaviour and sow the seeds of criminal activity. Alienation and congestion are particularly evident in urban areas, county towns and holiday resorts. This is causing some Travellers to take to the travelling life once again because, they argue, it is healthier and preferable to life on the dole in urban Traveller ghettos. More worrying still, the alienation and oppression of Travellers over recent decades has been so intense that Travellers themselves are beginning to internalise feelings of inferiority. This is not unlike the internalisation of inferiority complexes in Asian and Black communities in mainland Europe. In Ireland it is causing many urban Travellers in particular to turn to alcohol and anti-social behaviour, which in turn exacerbates tensions between Travellers and the settled population.

Pilot surveys of the health status of Travellers reveal that they have significantly lower life-expectancy rates and much higher fertility rates than the national population. These surveys are far more important for those concerned with Traveller welfare issues than the national population census. They literally monitor the health of one of the most unhealthy and neglected groups in this country. For that reason alone they should be carried out on a regular basis in order to measure progress in the struggle against the health and social problems of the Traveller population. A pioneering survey of Traveller health carried out in 1987 found that the crude birth rate for Travellers was 34.9 per 1,000 births compared to a national figure of 16.6 per 1,000. Irish Travellers have one of the highest birth rates in the European Union. Fertility is particularly high among unhoused Travellers, especially among young Traveller families living on roadsides and in unserviced sites. The 1987 survey also found that the fertility rate for teenage Travellers living along the roadside may be seven times higher than it is among the housed population. Moreover, despite popular images to the contrary, the number of children born outside marriage is extremely low for the Traveller population. Of the 557 Traveller babies enumerated in the 1987 survey, only 19 (3.4%) were born outside marriage. This was one third of the national figure for births outside marriage. On the other hand, the incidence of still-birth is much higher in the travelling community than in the settled population. It was as high as 19.5 per 1,000 live births for Travellers in 1987 compared with the national figure of 6.9 per 1,000 for the settled population. Infant mortality was also sig-

Table 7: Mortality in early life for Travellers and 'settled' population in Ireland, 1987.

	'Settled' Pop.	Travellers
Stillbirth Rate (per 1,000 total births)	6.9	19.5
Perinatal Mortality Rate (per 1,000 total births)	9.9	28.3
Infant Mortality Rate (per 1,000 live births)	7.4	18.1

Source: Barry, Herrity and Solan, 1987.

nificantly higher among Travellers. It was 18.1 per 1,000 live births compared to the national figure of 7.4.[79] This is obviously partially linked to differentials in the level of antenatal care among Travellers and the national population. In O'Nualláin and Forde's survey of a Traveller community in the west of Ireland, one fifth of all mothers had visited a doctor less than three times during pregnancy. Less than one third had six or more visits.[80] This survey also revealed an extremely high incidence of birth difficulties among Travellers, particularly among the unhoused. Sixteen per cent of all births in their survey were premature and as many as forty per cent of Traveller mothers had experienced four or more miscarriages. Among the factors that contribute to such high rates of miscarriage and infant mortality are inadequate antenatal health-care, maternal malnutrition during pregnancy, recurrent pregnancies with short intervals between each one and poor accommodation and housing for Traveller mothers. As with Third World mothers who experience similar problems, these high incidences of miscarriage and infant mortality are clearly avoidable through proper antenatal health care and through improvements in Traveller accommodation and life-style.

Table 8: Marital status of female Travellers aged 15–24, 1981.*

Age	Single	Per cent	Married	Per cent
15	204	100%	0	0%
16	183	97.3%	5	2.7%
17	145	81.9%	32	18.1%
18	112	74.7%	37	24.7%
19	72	55.0%	57	43.5%
20	52	46.0%	60	53.1%
21	34	29.6%	80	69.6%
22	27	22.1%	89	73.0%
23	20	20.0%	71	74.0%
24	19	16.7%	92	80.7%

Source: Report of Travelling People Review Body, 1983.

* Widowed Travellers account for discrepancies in rows which do not amount to 100%.

Life expectancy for male Travellers in the late Eighties was also ten years less than the settled males. Life expectancy of female Travellers is twelve years less than that of the settled female population. As Figure 1 shows, the population pyramids for Travellers and for the national population are quite different. Indeed, the age structure of Irish Travellers is very similar to the age structures of poorer Latin American countries in the 1980s. In 1981, fifty-five per cent of the Traveller population was under fifteen years of age. The corresponding figure for the national population two years previous to this was only thirty per cent. In contrast to this, only 2.5 per cent of all Travellers were over sixty, compared to 14.9 per cent of the settled population. Only 1.6 per cent of Travellers who lived by the roadside were over sixty.[81] As the Travellers Health Status Study of 1987 showed, Irish Travellers now have life expectancies that the settled population had in the 1940s. In an editorial in the *Irish Times* it was suggested that the most damning indictment of the treatment of Travellers in this country was the fact that ninety-five per cent of them still die before the age of fifty-five.[82] The Travellers Health Status Study also showed that Travellers of all ages have far higher mortality rates than the national population and suggested that the rates were especially high among unhoused and poor Travellers. In a survey of the age at death of eighty-four Travellers in the early 1980s, it was found that twenty-two per cent died before they reached their twenty-fifth birthday.[83] Just under one fifth of all Traveller deaths in this survey were of children under five. It also showed that the very high rates of metabolic and congenital disorders among Travellers were partly explained by the practice of Travellers marrying within their own community. The picture that emerged from this report painted Travellers as a group who married young and had large families. In the early 1980s, over eighty per cent of travelling women aged 15–44 in the Dublin area were married. The corresponding figure for women in this age group in the national population was just under fifty-eight per cent (See Table 9). From birth to old age they have significantly higher mortality rates than the national population. Death from accidents and from

Table 9: Marriage and fertility among Travellers and general population, 1981.

Age Group	Dublin Travellers 1977	All Travellers 1981	National Population 1979
Married women aged 15–44 as % of all married women	82	74.8	58
Married women aged 15–44 as % of all women	75	61.5	54

Source: Report of Travelling People Review Body, 1983.

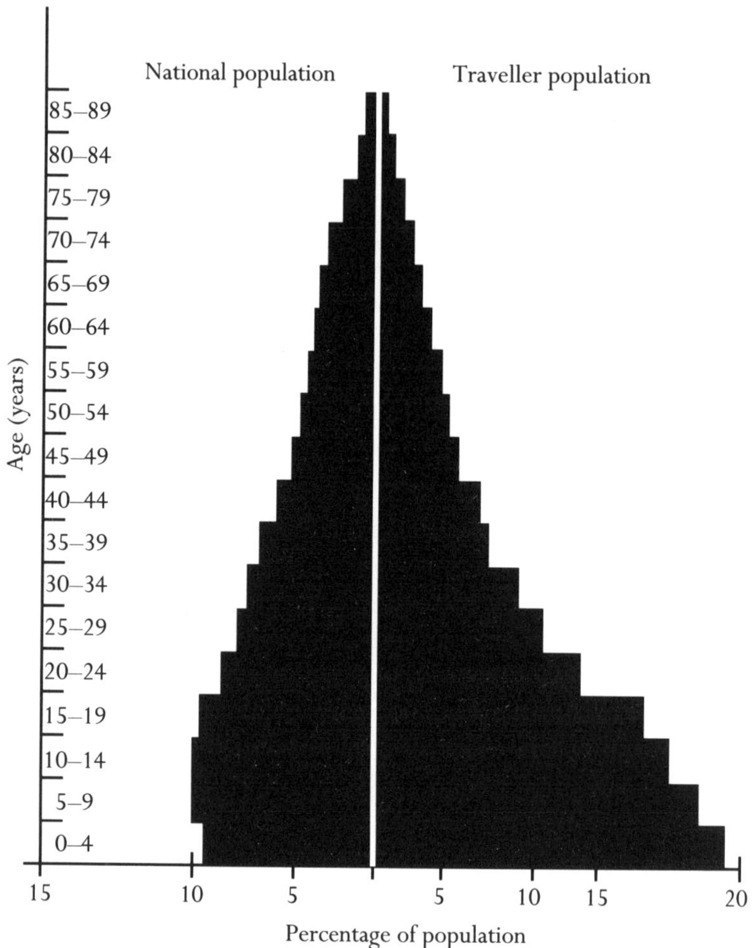

Source: Barry and Daly, 1988

Fig. 2: Traveller population, 1960–1994.

metabolic and congenital disorders were especially high among the Traveller population. The latter was certainly aggravated by the high incidence of consanguinity among Irish Travellers. In their detailed case study of a Traveller community in the west of Ireland, O'Nualláin and Forde found that almost two thirds of married couples claimed that they were related.[84] Thirty per cent of Traveller marriages in this study were between first cousins. A further twenty-four per cent were marriages between second cousins. Consanguinity in turn contributed to genetic disorders among Traveller children, many of whom are particularly prone to Hurlers Syndrome, a progressive metabolic disorder that can end in infantile death, blindness at an early age, hearing impairments and brittle bone diseases. As O'Nualláin and Forde convincingly argue, rates of metabolic and congenital disorders have probably increased as Travellers have settled down and married within their own restricted community. In former times, when Travellers were far more mobile and more widely dispersed throughout the country, it is likely that they chose their partners from a correspondingly larger and wider population. More recently, they argue, settled Travellers usually choose their partners from small localised communities. This has the effect of reducing the gene pool and increasing the degree of consanguinity among urban Travellers. The incidence of genetic and metabolic disorders among Traveller children today has probably increased as a result of the transition from nomadic rural to settled urban lifestyles. As O'Nualláin and Forde also point out, there is no easy solution to these problems. They are not only the product of in-group marriages among the Traveller population. They stem also from the practice of social closure which effectively shuts Travellers out of settled society, literally pushing them to the edges of society and to the lowest rungs of the social hierarchy. Thus these problems will not be solved while Travellers continue to marry within their own cousinhoods. This in turn is partly a repsonse to virulent anti-Traveller racism which makes it difficult

Table 10: Relationships between related marriage partners in a selected Traveller community in the west of Ireland, 1988.

Degree of Consanguinity	No. of couples	Percentage
First cousins	5	29.4
First cousins once removed	1	5.9
Second cousins	4	23.5
Second cousins once removed	5	29.4
Other relationships	2	11.8
Totals	17	100

Source: O'Nualláin and Forde, *Changing Needs of Irish Travellers* (Galway: Woodlands Centre 1992) p. 33.

for Travellers to integrate into the settled population even if they want to and it may well be exacerbated by efforts on the part of Travellers to preserve their own ethnic identity by marrying their own kind.

Traveller families living on the roadside clearly are the worst-off of all Travellers. They have even higher mortality rates than settled Travellers and the number of fatal accidents among the female Traveller population is also higher than in the settled Traveller community. Fifty per cent of all Travellers in Ireland today are in Cork, Dublin, Galway and Limerick. The Department of the Environment's Statistics on Travellers in Ireland reveal that just under half of all Travellers are housed today. Forty-two per cent of all Traveller families are in standard housing and a further six per cent are in group chalets.[85] Another study showed that there are just over 650 Traveller families with approximately 2,700 children under eighteen years in the Greater Dublin area alone. This figure does not include Traveller families living in local authority housing. Of these, 26.5 per cent are on the roadside, twenty-five per cent are in permanent serviced

Table 11: Traveller accommodation* in the Greater Dublin area 1994.

Living Condition	No. Families	Percentage
Roadside	173	26.5
Group housing	119	18.0
Permanent serviced sites	161	25.0
Temporary official sites	199	30.5
Total number families	652	100

Source: *Still No Place to Go*, 1994.

* Families in standard housing not included.

halting sites and just over thirty per cent are in temporary official sites with minimal facilities.[86] Fingal County Council area had 213 families in March 1994. This represented one third of all Travellers in the Greater Dublin area in that year. Thirty-six per cent of these were on the roadisde, 51.2 per cent were in temporary halting sites and only 27 families, thirteen per cent of the total, were in permanent serviced halting sites. Dun Laoghaire and Rathdown had ten per cent of Traveller families in the Dublin area. Fifty-four per cent of these were in group housing, 16.6 per cent were on permanent official sites and twenty-four per cent were on the roadside. Most young Travellers brought up in houses subsequently revert to trailers and caravans after they marry. As Fintan O'Toole recently argued, those living on the roadside and on unserviced sites were living in 'conditions, not of nomads, but of refugees'. He further suggested that:

> These conditions in and of themselves produce anger, disorder and disorder with settled people. In some parts of Dublin, local officials will only visit these sites with expensively hired security guards in tow. And herded into these dirty, ugly, isolated and unhappy squatter

> camps, the travellers themselves become easy targets for self-appointed vigilantes. The herding together of travellers of different families is itself creating hysteria . . . Families who have no connection with each other, and no particular desire to live together are moved against their will on to ugly and ill-prepared sites.[87]

A resident on one of these sites at Dunsink, located 'right beside the dump', stated:

> There is one toilet for 38 people and the skip is emptied every two months. There is no electricity and no safe place for children to play. The shops are about two miles away along a dangerous road.[88]

Table 12: Living conditions of Travellers in Greater Dublin area 1994.

Facility	No. of Traveller Families	Percentage
No flush toilet	231	36
No toilets	180	28
No electricity	345	53
No bath or shower	345	53
No refuse collection	60	10
Cold water only	345	53
No water supply	101	16
No public phone on site	652	100
No fire precautions	376	58
Space set aside for scrap	33	5

Source: *Still No Place to Go*, 1994.

Another writer described conditions on a Traveller encampment as follows:

> Rats eat holes in the floor. For washing and cooking, the family have to use one cold tap, which they share with thirty other people. The children are regularly ill with colds and chest infections. A neighbour's seven-day-old baby has just been rushed to hospital suffering from a disease its mother can't even pronounce. There is one toilet for every twelve people. A rusty skip is overflowing with domestic rubbish. It could be Sarajevo or Grozny, but it's Mulhuddart in north county Dublin.[89]

Ever since the early Sixties, studies have regularly linked together overcrowding, ill-health, high rates of infant mortality and the unhygienic conditions in unserviced halting sites and roadside encampments. Roadside families are obviously at greater risk because of traffic accidents and, more recently, because of vigilante-type attacks from elements in the settled community. Many injuries and deaths are also linked to caravan fires and inadequate fire-fighting equipment on both serviced and unserviced sites. The Dublin Travellers Educational and Development Group regularly point out that the actual number of families living in such conditions is extremely small even compared to the number of local authority waiting lists in the Greater Dublin area. Traveller activists insist that these families could all be satisfactorily accommodated quickly if the political will to do so existed.[90] Instead, large numbers of Travellers are forced to live in encampments not unlike the 'spontaneous settlements' that mushroomed around the capital of Nicaragua in the early years of Sandinista rule, except that, unlike Managua's shanty towns, Traveller encampments in the Dublin area are not the product of movement from one part of the city to the other. They are produced by families moving to the capital from the countryside and from other towns and cities.[91] Travellers gravitate to the capital for the same reasons as the settled population. They are also pushed towards cities because of the rise of anti-Traveller prejudice and social transformations in the countryside. Thus Travellers move to the city because they find rural areas increasingly inhospitable and because of the effectiveness of the 'boulder policy' adopted by local authorities to keep Travellers from settling along country roads and on the edges of Irish towns and villages. They are attracted to Dublin by work opportunities, leisure facilities and by the benefits associated with urban life. However, in comparision with the settled population, a smaller proportion of Travellers are in the capital city. Nevertheless, Traveller activists are worried that more and more Travellers in the Dublin area will be accommodated in unserviced 'temporary' official sites that will become 'permanent'. They also point to the fact that the recent break-up of the Dublin County Council into three local authority areas has cast doubt over the site programme to be adopted. Although the new authorities created in the wake of the break-up are currently carrying out surveys of Traveller accommodation in their areas, it is not clear whether they consider themselves bound to deliver on previously agreed programmes for solving the accommodation needs of Dublin Travellers. The programme for Government adopted in 1993 made a commitment to have Dublin Travellers accommodated by the year 2000. The Minister for local Government also announced that local authorities who do not make provision for Travellers will have their housing budgets cut. The Dublin Accommodation Coalition with Travellers (DACT) points to the fact that these commitments have still to be realised. They also argue that plans already exist to refurbish a number of official sites around the city but still no work has been done in many of the most run-down sites. They believe that local authorities, especially in the Dublin area, will increasingly resort to large temporary sites as *ad hoc* solutions to the housing needs of urban Travellers. As past experience has shown, these are the very sites that exacerbate the health and social problems of Travellers. They also exacerbate racial tension between Travellers and the settled community.

To solve the most pressing problems facing Travellers in the capital, the Dublin Accommodation Coalition with Travellers made the following recommendations in March, 1994:

(1) Setting up of Traveller Accommodation Agency as recommended in the Interim Report of the Task Force on Travelling People in February 1994.

(2) Creation of more transient sites with good quality facilities.

(3) Department of Environment should give grants for maintenance and upgrading of permanent sites and group housing scheme.

(4) Existing temporary sites should be upgraded where appropriate to permanent sites in consultation with Traveller residents.

(5) Moratorium on all evictions and forced movement of Travellers.

(6) Emergency provision of basic facilities for families camped illegally on roadside until permanent accommodation is provided.

(7) Contracts for site development to include timescales for completion of sites and penalties to be imposed for delayed completions.

(8) Traveller sites to be integrated into local environment and to be of good quality design. Financial penalties for local authorities who fail to provide good quality, culturally appropriate accommodation for Travellers in their area.

(9) Recognition that Travellers are an ethnic minority and that nomadic lifestyle needs to be translated into practical action through consultation with Travellers.

(10) Statutory bodies with responsibility for providing accommodation for Travellers should co-operate with Travellers and their organisations.

(11) Plan for future Traveller population growth in Dublin area.

(12) Statutory bodies to confront racist attitudes towards Travellers.

(13) Commitment to allow for Traveller participation in design, planning and maintenance of sites.

Irish Travellers have not only been victims of historical neglect. As we have already seen, they are also the victims of social and structural change in rural society. The decline of mixed small farming communities since the 1960s, together with the rise of powerful agribusiness interests have particularly contributed to the shrinking of the social and geographical space within which Travellers traditionally manoeuvred. The social distance separating Travellers from settled communities has also widened from the 1960s onwards. This in turn has led to the erosion of social tolerances which allowed 'tinkers' to live side by side with settled communities in post-independence Ireland. Thus traditional public rights-of-way were blocked; fields were more carefully fenced; a 'boulder policy' was adopted to prevent Travellers camping at traditional roadside halting sites, and the Gardaí, often acting under pressure from local business interests, moved 'tinkers' along so that they would not disrupt business life and traffic. As Ireland adopted an 'open door' policy for encouraging the diversification and dispersal of industry, 'tinkers' were seen as a social nuisance in urban and rural areas. By the Seventies and Eighties, they were widely considered to be troubling the peace and jeopardising the prosperity of town and countryside alike. As they moved from declining small farming regions into Dublin, Limerick, and Cork, their encampments increased in size and number. Many local authorities now worried that Traveller settlements were becoming permanent fixtures on the landscape. Others feared that they were damaging the image of Ireland as a modern and progressive society.

The traditional links between Travellers and small farming communities that characterised Traveller relations with the settled population since the nineteenth century also collapsed at this time.

Table 13: Percentage Traveller households in roadside caravans by county in Ireland in 1986.

County	Percentage	
Wicklow	61.8	
Kildare	71.9	
Leitrim	47.1	
Tipperary North	40.6	
Limerick	39.7	
Roscommon	38.6	
Laois	36.4	
Cavan	36.0	Above National Average
Clare	31.7	
Cork	30.7	
Carlow	29.6	
Tipperary South	29.3	
Meath	28.6	
Kilkenny	27.3	
Donegal	26.2	
Offaly	24.4	
Galway	23.7	
Dublin	21.3	
Longford	21.8	
Louth	21.8	
Wexford	19.1	
Waterford	17.2	Below National Average
Monaghan	12.1	
Westmeath	9.8	
Kerry	8.1	
Mayo	8.0	
Sligo	4.8	
National Average =	25.7	

Source: Barry and Daly, 1988.

In their wake, contacts of a more narrowly specialised nature developed. This was especially noticeable in Dublin, Cork, Limerick and Galway where Travellers had to learn new skills and carve out new niches in an increasingly hostile urban environment. The fact that so many Travellers who moved to the larger cities ended up on welfare support confirmed an urban image of modern Irish Travellers as social misfits who were pathologically rapacious and psychologically egocentric. Indeed, the persistence of the 'Travelling life' well into the twentieth century was also considered by many as a form of 'class theft'.[92] As the last relics of a nineteenth-century counter-hegemonic rural culture which largely disappeared in the post-Famine decades, Travellers were viewed as an 'unmeltable' social bloc that had no place in modern Ireland. Their very ability to survive was considered a threat to hegemonic notions of respectability, work and property. Similarly, their refusal to assimilate, together with their dependence on social welfare, was taken by many to mean that traditional and 'respectable' 'tinkers' were now transformed into modern 'dole-spongers'. In the event Travellers were looked upon as a modern version of the 'undeserving poor'.

The rise of the welfare state also meant that charity towards Travellers also had little or no social meaning for the majority of Irish people. As recipients of welfare, Travellers who sought to supplement 'the dole' through begging were regarded as dishonest, despite the fact that they often benefited far less from the welfare state than the long-term unemployed and other disadvantaged groups. Steadman-Jones has shown that charity, the act of making a 'gift' to the 'deserving poor', serves important status-maintaining functions in many societies. Social anthropologists have identified three such functions. In the first place, the 'gift' has long had sacrificial connotations in societies where gifts were made to a deity. Weber pointed out that this form of generalised giving had significant implications for the recipients of charity. Thus, he argued, the individual for whom the sacrifice is made 'is regarded in the final analysis as unimportant'.[93] Human beings, in other words, are simply people whom one happens to encounter along the way. They have significance only because of their needs and solicitations. This precisely characterises social relations between Travellers and the settled population in the new Ireland that was forged in the Lemass years. In the new Ireland, the forms of charity discussed by Weber now defined Ireland's relationship with its missionary world overseas, not with its own poor at home. Indeed, in the post-War period, significant amounts of 'aid' were channeled through Catholic charities and the Catholic Church to Irish missionaries overseas. As Reagan suggests, this kind of generosity was not only part and parcel of an essentially 'spiritual rather than material relationship' – it also 'explains why that generosity can remain firmly locked in the charity rather than the solidarity mode'.[94] Travellers generally lost out more than most as a result of this geographical extension of charity to the 'unfortunate poor' overseas. They became the neglected poor at home. Settled people justified their neglect of Travellers and their refusal to give charity to beggars on Irish streets on the grounds that Ireland's poor, especially Travellers, were already supported through the welfare state. They also argued that, anyway, Travellers were much better-off than the more 'deserving' missionary poor.

Anthropologists have also shown that, in nearly all societies, regardless of the extent of disinterest in the poor, the giving of gifts conferred prestige on the giver. 'To give,' Marcel Mauss once wrote, 'is to show one's superiority.'[95] This aspect of charity also lost all social meaning with the rise of the Irish welfare state. Having racialised Travellers and transformed them into the social inferiors of even the most inferior in Irish society, most people had little need to prove their social superiority by giving alms to the travelling poor. Finally, as Steadman-Jones has argued, giving gifts has generally imposed obligations upon the receiver in that 'in order to receive one must behave in an acceptable manner, if only expressing gratitude and humility'.[96] In contemporary Ireland, and many other parts of Europe, this form of giving was depersonalised and made redundant with the rise of the welfare state. In circumstances where geographical gulfs separated rich and poor, particularly where they separated 'disrespectful' Travellers from 'respectable' settled people, the opportunities for giving in the traditional sense, and the benefits accruing from giving, were greatly diminished. The progressive separation of Travellers from settled society deformed social contact between the two populations and contributed to the deformation of Traveller society. As we have already seen, ever since the 1950s, large numbers of Travellers have increasingly found themselves in an alien world of expanding cities and rationalised agriculture. This is a world apart from the small mixed farming environment and rural communities formerly serviced by Irish Travellers. As we have also already seen, the high degree of Traveller dependence upon welfare caused many in the settled community to regard Travellers as lacking in the virtues of work and the settled life.

Their urbanisation confronted Travellers with new problems. On the one hand, life in the city was a constant effort to adapt as it became an unending struggle for survival in a new environment. On the other hand, most settled people felt that it was irresponsible to 'pamper' Travellers by extending charity towards them. For many others, Travellers were parochial and superstitious, a shameful memento of Ireland's historical disunity and a divisive force in Irish society. For the more extreme the survival of 'Tinkerism' suggested:

> . . . Ireland's inadequacy to international equity in the future. Since such equity demanded of the nation habits of industry, regimentation, and capitalistic self-improvement which the Tinkers, who represented a certain immutable Irishness, could not learn, then these habits might be beyond the reach of all Irish.[97]

4. The Geography of Closure and the Politics of Exclusion

The very openness of the Irish economy since the 1960s is in sharp contrast to the closed nature of Irish society. This has had serious implications for the survival of Traveller culture and indeed Traveller communities. As Ireland developed into an exceptionally open *economy*, it developed many of the characteristics of an extremely closed *society*. This is nowhere more noticeable than in contemporary attitudes towards Irish Travellers. It is also reflected in the status of Traveller issues in Irish political discourse. Thus the very terms that we use in addressing Traveller issues effectively close them out of respectable political discourse. Terms like 'knackers', 'itinerants' and 'gypos' debase Travellers to the level of a racial minority. This debasement is especially noticeable in the political arena where the very idea of Travellers' rights and the Traveller vote is anathema to the majority of local and national politicians.[98] Apart from the notable exceptions of Liz Mc Manus, Mary Robinson, Emmet Stagg, Mervyn Taylor and the small handful of politicans who have given support to the Task Force on the Travelling Community set up in 1973, most political leaders in this country collude in the criminalisation of Traveller practices. They tacitly and actively support the 'boulder policy' which prevents Travellers from settling in traditional halting sites and refuse to meet their most basic demands for health care and educational reform to meet the needs of travelling people.

At national level, this new politics of exclusion has given rise to a geography of closure which has sought to exclude the 'foreigner' from 'Fortress Ireland' and 'foreign practices' from Catholic nationalist Ireland. Moreover, the rise of anti-Traveller prejudice in post-Thatcherite Britain has meant that traditional Irish Travellers and

New Age Travellers are increasingly forced out of British towns and cities into Ireland. In many respects this geography of closure, and its accompanying politics of exclusion, may be regarded as Irish and British variants of the resurgent 'blood and soil' nationalisms emerging elsewhere in Europe.[99] It is having particularly disturbing effects on the settled population's relations with disadvantaged communities, especially Travellers and New Age Travellers. It is also affecting Irish relationships with Third World countries. On the one hand, it cultivates a 'Fortress Ireland' mentality which rationalises the exclusion of 'foreigners' from Irish society – except those (e.g. overseas investors, foreign visitors, property speculators and fee-paying students) who can enhance our political and economic position by investing in Ireland or by promoting Irish interests abroad. Thus, despite the fact that it has consistently relied on *other countries* to host its 'surplus' sons and daughters, the Irish state rigorously polices migration routes into Ireland. It also discriminates against immigrants and asylum seekers from the 'wrong side' of the colour bar or from countries with which the Irish government has no vested interest in maintaining good relations.

At a more local level, the politics of exclusion is nurturing new closures in urban and rural communities throughout Ireland. This is creating biological constructs of community as 'kith and kin' – single class and even corporate entities which literally seek to relegate Travellers and New Age Travellers to the edges of Irish society. At the local level also, such quasi-biological constructs of community, particularly where they fuse with the proprietorial pride of place of urban and rural communities, have been responsible for the construction of places as sites of ownership and control.[100] In towns as far apart as Bantry, Bray, Glenamaddy, Navan, Tuam and Enniscorthy, this has given rise to new strategies of social closure, including violent crusades to prevent Travellers from despoiling areas of scenic beauty and to prevent them from settling within rural middle-class and working-class communities.[101]

There were widespread accusations that an urban gang was hired to wreck the caravans of a couple of Traveller families living close to the shore at Bantry. Also a social welfare officer in the town was censured for portraying local Travellers as work-shy.[102] In towns like Bantry, Bray, Glenamaddy, Moate and Navan, Travellers have come to represent racialised 'outsiders'. Their social behaviour and lifestyles – not those of their attackers – are used to evoke images of chaos, violence and disorder. This has caused Mc Veigh to suggest that the very term 'community' has become a problematic and exclusive notion in contemporary Ireland.[103] It often lies at the very heart of the many conflicts currently being waged between settled communities and Travellers. Moreover, unlike in earlier decades when 'tinkers' performed important functions and literally found a place among rural and working-class communities, communities in contemporary Ireland are contested terrains where the reception accorded Travellers depends on the outcome of local battles waged between the forces of tolerance and the increasingly well-organised forces of intolerance.

Keeping travellers on the move has become a national obsession in Ireland. One local councillor recently suggested that if Irish travellers wanted their ethnicity, they 'should go and get it somewhere else'. Another suggested that the very idea of building more serviced halting grounds for Travellers in Ireland today was nothing short of 'a ridiculous crusade to cover Ireland with holiday camps'. 'Cleaning travellers out' of working-class districts, and their removal from the edges of our cities and country towns, have become acceptable principles of Irish political culture. This form of 'ethnic cleansing' should be as unacceptable here as it is elsewhere in Europe.

Mc Veigh has shown how there has long been a pre-existing organic anti-Traveller racism in Ireland which has little to do with learned racial behaviour imported from Britain, the United States and Europe. One Belfast Traveller activist recently defined this genre of racism as:

> . . . a practice that labels the culture of the travellers as deviance and seeks to impose the values of the dominant group on the Travellers. It is a practice that creates negative stereotypes of the Traveller and seeks to interpret the Travellers on the basis of such stereotypes.[104]

As Mc Veigh suggests, this kind of racism has become:

> . . . a central means by which tensions are symbolically transferred from inside the community to the outside. Thus – through a convenient sublimation – people inside the community are not sexually active, Black people are; people inside the community do not exploit their fellows, Jewish people do; men inside the community are not violent to their partners, Travelling men are. In pathologising the 'out-group', the 'community' de-pathologises itself. This process is obviously negative for the 'out-group' in that it encourages discrimination and violence against them to ensure that they stay the 'out-group'.[105]

This means that anti-Traveller prejudice today is not only racist in character – it is also at the root of the social, economic and geographical exclusion of Travellers from Irish society. This type of anti-Traveller racism is rooted in a belief that the way of life of settled people is the modern norm and that the way of life of Travellers is a throw-back to less civilised times that are best forgotten in a modern society like Ireland.[106] The level of racism and the degree of anti-Traveller exclusion are extremely high. They are often justified in racist terms reminiscent of classical nineteenth-century racism. Thus Court suggests that:

> The terms dirty and clean and alternately black and white have been used in many social contexts, including the Irish one, to designate outsiders and insiders. Tinkers, for example, have frequently been called black

> by Gypsies as well as by settled Irish, two peoples who were themselves named black and dirty by the English. The black or dirty person in these instances is one who is not entitled to full participation in the institutions that embody the vital, moral structures of the given society, one who is denied its membership and protection.[107]

This type of anti-Traveller racism has become particularly virulent since the 1970s. It is especially noticeable in urban areas and country towns that were widely held to be 'under siege' from Travellers, including, more recently, New Age Travellers.[108] It is also a feature of community life in the richer agricultural counties in the midlands and the east coast, and in 'gentrified' tourist resorts where the presence of Travellers is interpreted as a threat to the economic well-being of local communities.[109]

Anti-Traveller racism is deeply embedded in the social fabric and agrarian history of Ireland. Since the Sixties it has also acquired new adherents in urban centres, towns and villages throughout the country. The roots of this racism are to be found in a persistent post-Famine 'common sense', social Darwinism which insisted that only the strongest should inherit the earth. The meek, ironically, would come into their inheritance in a post-earthly existence. As I have already argued, anti-Traveller and 'anti-tinker' racism is also traceable to a late nineteenth- and twentieth-century rural fundamentalism which prioritised the values of property-owners over and above those of the propertyless. There is a marked overlap between anti-Traveller racism and nationalism in Ireland which goes back to the circumstances in which the Irish nation was conceived as a cradle for bourgeois and petty bourgeois respectability. On the one hand, Irish nationalism, simply considered as a struggle for the control of territory, has striven to control population and to produce an Irish 'people' as a political community.[110] On the other hand, the Irish nation was forged as an historical system of exclusions and dominations. It became a place where the patriarchal values of the rural bourgeoisie occupied pride of place, a place where Irish women were accorded positions as second-class citizens, a place where the child in the womb had rights over and above its mother, a place, finally, where Travellers were scarcely even considered as citizens and were viewed instead as wards of the state.

More recently a newer politics of exclusion has emerged which is nurturing new closures in urban and rural communities throughout Ireland. This is creating biological constructs of community as 'kith and kin' or single-class entities which literally seek to relegate Travellers to the edges of Irish society. This has given rise to new strategies of social closure, including violent crusades to prevent Travellers from 'despoiling' areas of scenic beauty and obstructing their attempts to settle within rural, middle-class and working-class communities. The exclusion of Travellers from working-class and middle-class areas is so complete in Ireland today that it compares with some of the most radical exclusions of Islamic minorities in mainland Europe and of Black and Hispanic communities in the United States. Indeed, in Ireland the treatment of travelling people is often worse than in many other European countries. In the Czech Republic, President Vaclav Havel recently inaugurated a monument to some 5,600 Gypsies who were either killed or transported to Auschwitz. Although the Nazis had been responsible for setting up two special concentration camps where Czechoslovak Gypsies were interned, these were run by Czech and Slovak guards.[111] In Czechoslovakia, as in other east European countries, the reason why the suffering of Gypsies went unnoticed was because they were not considered an integral part of eastern European nation-states. This has gradually been redressed in recent years as these countries seek to atone for their wartime treatment of Gypsies and other Travellers. In Hungary, for example, Gypsies have managed to retain many of their own customs. They literally dance to their own music, and Gypsy music, especially on the violin, has had a major impact on Hungarian music since the sixteenth century. In Hungary, as in Ireland, travelling people are banned from bars and other 'Gypsy-free zones'. However, Gypsies generally fare better in Hungary where the government at least includes them in a list of twelve minorities whose rights are to be protected through legislative reform. In Ireland's case, such legislative reform is only just beginning. It is also facing widespread opposition from publicans and others in the business community who seem determined to keep their premises 'tinker-free'.

Among other factors which have been encouraging anti-Traveller racism in Ireland today are the strength of community life in urban and rural Ireland, the reconstruction of Irish society under the hegemony of a Euro-centred bourgeoisie, and the intimate nature of community life in Ireland which makes it extremely difficult for 'strangers' to escape notice. In an increasingly sanitised landscape dominated by new business and professional elites, Travellers have also come to represent 'filth' and 'chaos'. The new political managers in these areas often look on Travellers simply as social problems to be dealt with, usually by whatever means that work. Racial categorisations of Travellers as 'filthy outsiders' flourish in such environments.

This is reflected in attitudes to the 'Traveller problem' in Ireland today. One recent survey found that six adults out of ten would object to a halting site being built by local authorities within a quarter of a mile of their homes.[112] The urban middle classes – those furthest removed from Travellers – were among the least perturbed by the location of halting sites, with fifty per cent saying they would not object to Travellers locating within a quarter of a mile of them. Elsewhere, however, especially in county towns where Travellers have tried to settle, anti-Traveller crusading has reached unprecedented heights. This is also true of rural communities where, according to this survey, three quarters of all respondents objected to halting sites in their areas. This survey also found that the most favoured solution to the 'Traveller problem' was separate housing for travelling people. Sixty per cent of respondents favoured this option.

More than one half of the liberal, middle class claimed that they had no objection to Travellers settling near the settled community. The corresponding figure for the farming community was less than one third. Those between 18–21 years of age were the most in favour of more support for Traveller communities. Three quarters of the total targeted population believed that the Traveller lifestyle was something to be respected. However, the majority of those interviewed also felt that it was unreasonable for Travellers to want housing in the winter months and to have the choice of travelling in summertime. This survey not only stressed the ambiguity of Irish attitudes towards Travellers, it also stressed the closed nature of Irish community life and emphasised the social distance separating Travellers from all sections of the settled population. As one commentator argued:

> The truth is that Irish society does not want the intellectual discomfort of facing the facts when it comes to dealing with our travelling community. We do not want to baldly state what we really feel, namely that we disapprove of much of what happens in the context of the travelling lifestyle, from their migrant behaviour, halting sites close to settled communities, perceived lack of respect for law and order, and roadside trading. Instead we package those feelings in pious statements about respecting their different culture and neatly pass the buck by arguing that the authorities should find the appropriate solution.[113]

Because those with most choices in Irish society often choose to live only with 'their own kind', disadvantaged underclasses like Travellers are forced into urban wastelands that have few linkages with the working economy. Over the past few decades this has had the effect of excluding Travellers and other 'undesirables' from middle-class suburbs and gentrified rural and urban areas. It also

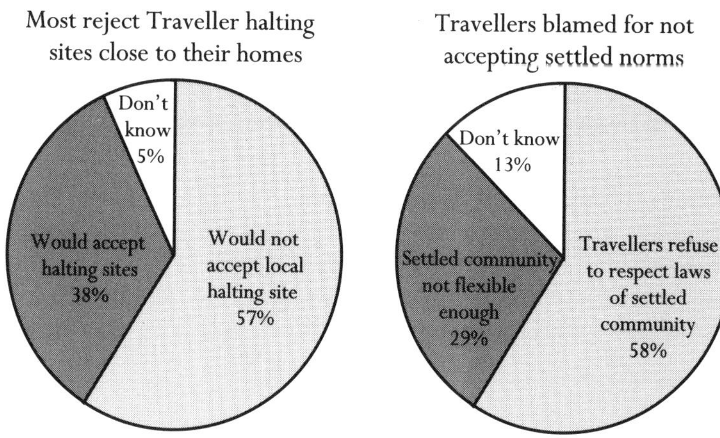

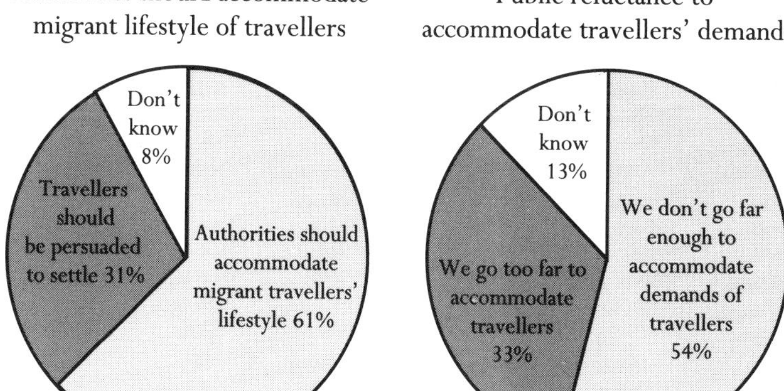

Source: *Sunday Independent*/Irish Marketing Survey, *Sunday Independent,* January 19, 1995.

Fig. 3: Irish Attitudes to Travellers, 1995

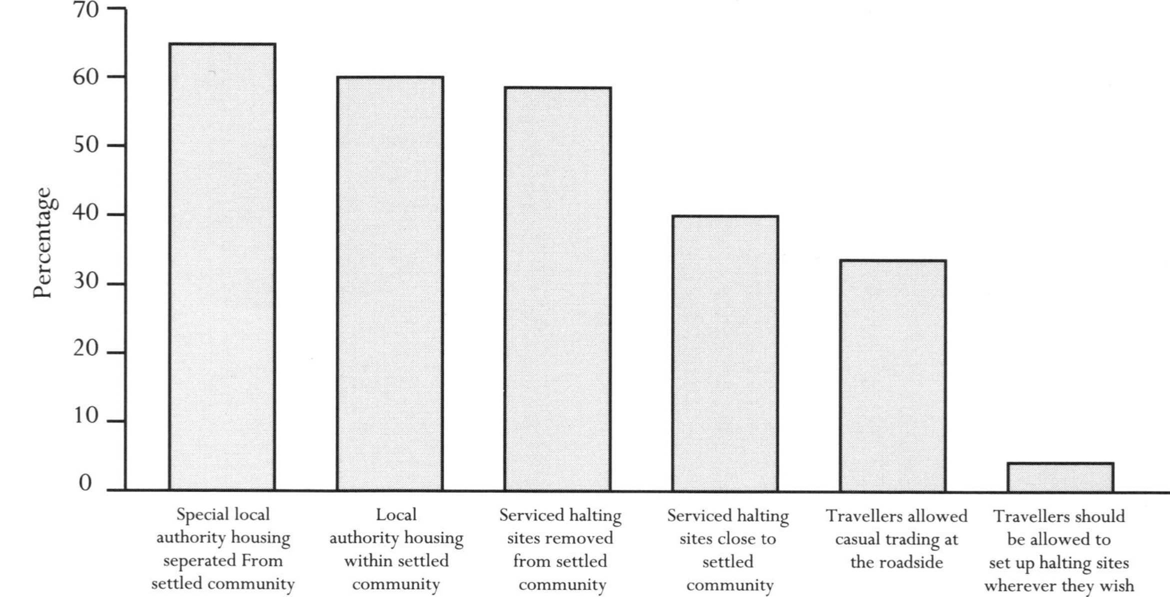

Source: *Sunday Independent*/Irish Marketing Survey, *Sunday Independent* January 19 1995.

Fig 4: Halting sites and casual trading by travellers seen as problems

tends to exclude them from the heart of working-class communities. This makes it extremely difficult for Travellers to carve a position for themselves in Irish society. The very layout of our cities, and the general conservatism of Irish politics, also make it extremely difficult for Travellers and other disadvantaged groups to develop any meaningful community-based politics to redress their socio-economic marginalisation. This is because the fragmentation of urban space, and the separation out of larger and larger disadvantaged areas from the working city, isolates better-off sectors from the less well-off in Irish society. It also hinders the social interaction needed to redress glaring social inequalities and cultural differences in Irish society. Indeed, the isolation of Travellers, and the fragmentation of their world, is reducing Travellers to the status of social outcasts in contemporary Ireland.

Despite the fact that the world of the Irish Traveller has been turned upside down in recent decades, not least by infrastructural developments which literally buried the networks which linked Travellers to the settled population, Irish Travellers have shown great skill in adapting to new circumstances. In many instances this has involved Travellers who were formerly settled taking to the road once again in order to improve their social and economic position, and to escape victimisation from the settled community. The marked increase in victimisation of travelling communities in recent years is also keeping Travellers on the move. Economic and political forces operating in inner-city areas are causing 'settled Travellers' to prioritise the travelling life once again, in preference to a life 'on the dole' in the 'slow lane' economy. Traveller families who take to the road and react against assimilation are behaving not unlike 'unmeltable' minorities elsewhere in Europe. This is especially true of countries where racial victimisation has caused the offspring of ethnic minorities to reconsider the terms of their assimilation into mainstream society and to defend their own cultural values.

CONCLUSION

Ireland has regularly capitalised on its colonial past to enhance its standing with Third World countries. This has allowed Irish people to pride themselves on their record as supporters of anti-colonial and anti-racist struggles. It also meant they could be deluded into thinking that Ireland was a non-racist society. Irish political discourse today is littered with the language of accommodation which stresses good neighbourliness, charity, tolerance and respect for national differences. This is particularly noticeable in the 'politics of the high moral plain' and in political discussions on Northern Ireland which constantly ask 'why can't these people get along each other', while simultaneously ignoring the high degree of social and political intolerance in Catholic Ireland. The isolation of Travellers, their 'parcelling out' among deprived urban communities and the fragmentation of their world is reducing Travellers to the position of social outcasts in contemporary Ireland. Local authorities in Dublin and the country in general look to this as a way of coping with Traveller issues and 'sharing the burden' of 'the Traveller problem'. Thus they look on Travellers as a 'problem community' to be shared out among the 'normal' population. This encourages anti-Traveller racism and exacerbates tensions between the Traveller and the national population. Local authorities also often 'hide' halting sites away from towns and cities and locate them in isolated areas away from shops, schools and community services. They particularly ignore Traveller preferences for small extended family sites and pay more attention to placating the majority population than addressing the needs of Travellers.

The fragmentation of the Travellers' world has a number of other problems. As Niall Crowley suggests, the 'sharing out' of Travellers among the electoral wards of large cities terminally weakens the Traveller vote.[114] It also means that Travellers find it extremely difficult to carve out a constituency on the Irish political landscape. This is reflected in the status of Traveller issues in Irish political discourse and in the very terms that we use in addressing Traveller issues which effectively closes them out of respectable political discourse. The widespread use of terms like 'knackers' and 'itinerants' reduces Travellers to the level of a racial minority. Their debasement is particularly obvious in the political arena where the very idea of Travellers having rights is something foreign to the majority of local and national politicians.

Despite the fact that the world of the Irish Traveller has been turned upside-down in recent decades, not least by infrastructural developments which literally buried the networks which linked Travellers to the settled population, Irish Travellers have shown great skill in adapting to new circumstances. Groups like the Dublin Travellers Educational and Development Group, the Cork Traveller Visibility Group, the Belfast Traveller Support Group, the Navan Traveller Group and the Tullamore Traveller Movement have argued that Travellers today are showing that they are no longer prepared to act as passive victims of Ku-Klux-Klan-type tactics or vigilante attacks. They have also interpreted the lack of public outcry against criminal attacks on isolated Traveller families as official collusion with powerful anti-Traveller elements who wish to either rid Ireland of Traveller communities or force them to assimilate, under the dominant culture's terms, into mainstream society.

There are clear parallels between anti-Traveller violence in Ireland and neo-fascist attacks on migrant workers elsewhere in Europe. However, unlike in Britain, France, Germany and Holland where neo-fascist violence has been widely condemned, virulent anti-Traveller racism in Ireland goes largely unheeded. Unlike these countries, Ireland has not witnessed any widespread, organised demonstrations by mainstream society against this type of racism. However, we have recently seen Travellers themselves taking to the streets on this issue. It could be argued that Traveller issues will be taken seriously in this country only when more of those from the settled community are literally prepared to join with Travellers in these demonstrations.

Instead, the obstructionist behaviour of local councillors fuels anti-Traveller racism in Ireland. Parties representative of propertied interest, particularly Fine Gael, have generally been more obstructionist than Labour councillors and the Democratic Left, although these parties also are not without their obstructionists.[115] This in turn is strengthening an already existing institutionalised anti-Traveller racism and encouraging the use of legal and *illegal* strategies for ensuring that Travellers literally find no place in Irish society. Moreover, because Travellers have little or no access to law-enforcing agencies, they are often compelled to defend themselves from violent attack. This perpetuates stereotypical images of Travellers as pathological trouble-makers who have no place in peaceful communities.

The upsurge of Traveller awareness groups under a leadership drawn from the Traveller community itself has done much to redress the devaluation of Traveller culture, both by the settled community, and, more damagingly, by Travellers themselves. The Italian Marxist Antonio Gramsci would have called this an 'organic intelligentsia'.[116] Drawn from the ranks of the Travellers themselves, it is articulating Traveller demands and, more importantly, raising the political and ethnic consciousness of the Traveller community. This is arguably the single most important development in Irish Traveller culture in this century. Thus Traveller activists like Chrissie O'Sullivan, Anne Doherty, Martin Collins, Helen Casey, Catherine Joyce, Davey Joyce, Michael Mc Donagh, Jimmy Power, Martin Joyce and many others have been re-evaluating the position of Travellers in Irish society and have been highlighting the legitimate demands of Travelling people. They are also severing links with paternalistic, charitable and church-based organisations which traditionally mediated between Travellers and the settled society. In valorising Traveller culture this new leadership has also been struggling against the internalisation of feelings of racial inferiority. In so doing, it has not only politicised and radicalised Traveller issues, it is also insisting that while the equal-status legislation about to be introduced will be of great benefit to the Traveller cause, it will be of little use to Travellers themselves unless it is accompanied by a tribunal to deal effectively with the very specific complaints of anti-Traveller discrimination and victimisation. As Mary Cummins, one journalist who has been covering Traveller issues since the 1980s, recently argued, this will require 'a magnificent sea-change' in parish after parish that would require residents and Travellers to sit down to air their very real grievances and discuss their equally obvious differences.[117] It will also require far more support from progressive elements in Irish society than has hitherto been given to the Travelling people.

References

1. Ibn Khaldoun, *The Muqaddiman* (London: Castle Press, 1958), p. 332.
2. Bruce Chatwin, *Songlines* (London: Picador, 1987), p. 218.
3. *No Place To Go* (Dublin: Irish Travellers Movement, 1992), p. 7.
4. Ibid., p. 15.
5. Bruce Chatwin, *Songlines* p. 45.
6. Ibid., p. 219.
7. Anthony Smith, *The Ethnic Origins of Nations* (London: Blackwell, 1986), p. 34.
8. Ibid., p. 35.
9. T. Acton, 'Categorising Irish Travellers', May Mc Cann et al. (eds) *Irish Travellers: Culture and Identity* (1994), p. 49.
10. Michael Simmons, 'Gypsies: Victims of Ethnic Cleansing', *The Guardian* (January 23, 1995).
11. Jim Mac Laughlin, 'Politics of exclusion lead to anti-Traveller racism', *The Cork Examiner* (November 29, 1994).
12. Cormac O'Grada, 'Seasonal migration and post-Famine adjustment in the west of Ireland, *Studia Hibernia*, vol. xxxiii (1973), pp. 45–69.
13. James E. Handley, *The Irish in Modern Scotland* (Cork: Cork University Press, 1947).
14. Dympna Mc Loughlin, 'Irish Travellers and ethnicity', *Irish Travellers: Gender and Identity* (1994), pp. 54–77.
15. A. Rao, (ed.) *The Other Nomads* (Cologne : Bohlau, 1987).
16. Sinéad Ní Shuinear, 'Irish Travellers and the Origins Question', *Irish Travellers: Gender and Identity* (1994), p. 55.
17. T. Acton, 'Categorising Irish Travellers' (1994), p. 49.

18. Bettina Barnes, 'Irish Travelling People', Fanrham Rehfrisch (ed.) *Gypsies, Tinkers and Other Travellers* (London : Academic Press, 1975), p. 232 .

19. T. Acton, 'Categorising Irish Travellers' (1994), p. 54.

20. Keith Thomas, *Religion and the Decline of Magic* (Harmondsworth: Pelican, 1984), p. 796.

21. D. Kenrick and G. Puxton, *The Destiny of European Gypsies* (London: Basic Books, 1994).

22. M. O'Reilly, *With Travellers – A Handbook for Teachers* (Blackrock Teachers Centre, Dublin, 1993).

23. J. Liegeois, *Gypsies and Travellers* (Strasbourg: Council of Europe Publications, 1987).

24. David Harvey, *Social Justice and The City* (London: Edward Arnold, 1973): also C. Wright Mills, *The Sociological Imagination* (London: Pelican, 1978).

25. Cailiosa Hickland, *Nomadism and Identity: The Case of the Irish Travellers* (M.A. Thesis, Department of Geography, University College Cork, 1994).

26. E. MacNeill, *Irish History* (Dublin: Macmillan, 1968), p. 34.

27. S. Gmelsch and G. Gmelsch, 'The Emergence of an Ethnic Group: The Irish Tinkers', *Anthropological Quarterly*, vol. 49, no. 4, pp. 225–38.

28. Ibid., p. 228.

29. T. Acton, ' Categorising Irish Travellers' (1994), p. 45.

30. J.P. Liegeois, *Gypsies* (London: Alsaqi Books, 1986).

31. Ní Shuinear, 'Irish Travellers and the Origins Question', p. 58.

32. Helen Lucy Burke, 'Some cultures are more respectable', *The Sunday Tribune* (April 2, 1995).

33. Robbie Mc Veigh, 'The Specificity of Irish Racism', *Race and Class*, Vol. 33 (1992) no. 4, pp. 31–45.

34. Hugo Grotius, *On the Origin of the Native Races of America* (Edinburgh: Shortwell, 1884), p. 57.

35. Ronald Meek, *Social Science and the Ignoble Savage* (London: Cambridge University Press, 1987), p.56.

36. Ibid., p. 5 .

37. Ellen Semple, *Influences of Geographic Environment: On the Basis of Ratzel's System of Anthropo-Geography* (London: Constable, 1911), p. 97.

38. L.P. Curtis, *Anglo-Saxons and Celts* (New York: Academic Press, 1967).

39. Ibid., p.71.

40. David Lloyd, *Anomalous States* (Dublin: Lilliput Press, 1993), p. 7; Frantz Fanon, *The Wretched of the Earth* (Harmondsworth: Pelican, 1984).

41. Artelia Court, *Puck of the Droms: The Lives and Literature of the Irish Tinkers* (Berkeley: University of California Press, 1987), p.16.

42. Jim Mac Laughlin, 'Defending the Frontiers: The Political Geography of Race and Racism in the European Community', Colin Williams (ed.) *The Political Geography of the New World Order* (London: Bellhaven Press, 1993), pp. 20–45.

43. A. Court, *Puck of the Droms*, p.1.

44. Jim Mac Laughlin, 'The Political geography of Nation-building and Nationalism in Social Sciences', *Political Geography Quarterly*, Vol.5. no. 4, pp. 299–329; Jim Mac Laughlin, 'Place, Politics and Culture in Nation-building Ulster', *Canadian Review of Studies in Nationalism*, 1986 Vol. XX, nos.1–2, pp.97–112; Benedict Anderson, *Imagined Communities: Refelctions on the Origins and Spread of Nationalism* (London: Verso Press, 1983).

45. G.R.C. Keep, 'Official Opinion on Irish Emigration in the later Nineteenth Century', *Irish Ecclesiastical Record*, Vol. lxxxi (1943), pp. 412–421.

46. J.M. Synge, *My Wallet of Photographs* (Dublin: Dolmen, 1971).

47. Terry Eagleton, *Heathcliff and the Great Hunger* (London: Verso, 1995).

48. David Greene and Edward Stephens, *J.M. Synge 1871–1909* (New York: Collier, 1961), p. 123.

49. Jim Mac Laughlin, 'State-centered social science and the anarchist critique', *Antipode, A Radical Journal of Geography*, Vol. 18, no. 1, 1986, pp. 11–38; Peter Kropotkin, *Anarchism: Its Philosophy and Ideal* (London: Freedom Press, 1896).

50. Terry Eagleton, *Heathcliff*, p. 313.

51. Fintan O'Toole, 'Tackling travellers issue key test for coalition', *The Irish Times*, December 23, 1994.

52. John B. Keane, *The Field* (Cork: Mercier, 1993).

53. Etienne Balibar and Immanuel Wallerstein *Race and Nation* (New York: Sage, 1991).

54. A. Court, *Puck of the Drom*, p. 1.

55. Ibid., p. 1.

56. Ibid., p. 2.

57. Declan Kiberd, 'The Elephant of Revolutionary Forgetfulness', Mairín Ní Dhonnchadha and Theo Dorgan (eds.) *Revising the Rising* (Dublin: New Island Publications, 1991).

58. A. Court, *Puck of the Droms*, p. 26.

59. Carlo Levi, *Christ Stopped at Eboli* (Harmondsworth: Penguin, 1982), p. 132.

60. B. Traven, *General From the Jungle* (London: Allison and Busby, 1983), pp. 128–29.

61. A. Court, *Puck of the Droms*, pp. 25–6.

62. *Report of the Commission on Itinerancy* (Dublin: Government Publications, 1963),: p. 23.

63. *Report of the Commission on Itinerancy* (1963).

64. Barnes, 'Irish Travelling People' (1975), p. 250.

65. Hickland, *Nomadism and Identity* (1994), p. 40.

66. Barnes, 'Irish Travelling People' (1975), p. 250.

67. Ibid., p. 252.

68. John O'Connell, 'Ethnicity and Irish Travellers', *Anti-Racist Law and the Travellers* (Dublin: Dublin Travellers Educational and Development Group, 1993), p. 11.

69. *Report of the Travelling People Review Body* (Dublin: The Stationery Office, 1983), pp.7–8.

70. O'Reilly, *Traveller Handbook*, p. 45.

71. *Report of the Travelling People Review Body*, p.11.

72. Ibid., p.49.

73. J. O'Flynn, *Identity Crisis* (London: Action Group for Irish Youth, 1993), p. 49.

74. Ibid., p. 50.

75. Ibid., p. 51.

76. *Report of the Commission on Itinerancy* (1963), p. 36.

77. Barnes, 'Irish Travelling People', p. 254.

78. *The Irish Times* (May 20, 1995).

79. Joseph Barry, Bernadette Herity, and Joseph Solan, *The Travellers' Health Status Study* (Dublin: Health Research Board, 1989), pp. 14–15.

80. Sinead O'Nualláin and Mary Forde, *Changing Needs of Irish Travellers* (Galway: Woodlands Centre, 1992), p. 49.

81. *Report of the Travelling People Review Body*, p. 92.

82. *The Irish Times* (May 20, 1995).

83. Barry, Herity, and Solan, *Travellers' Health Status Study*, p. 35.

84. O'Nualláin and Forde, *Changing Needs of Irish Travellers*, p.33.

85. Ibid., p. 22.

86. *Still No Place to Go* (Irish Traveller Movement, Dublin, 1994), p. 14.

87. Finton O'Toole, 'Tackling Traveller issue', 1994.

88. *No Place to Go* (1992), p.4.

89. Will Hanafin, 'Go, Move, Shift', *The Big Issue*, Dublin, Issue 14, March 16–29, 1995.

90. *No Place to Go* (1992).

91. Doreen Massey, *Nicaragua* (Milton Keynes: Open Univeriity Press, 1982).

92. Mc Veigh, *Irish Racism* (1992), p. 41.

93. M. Weber, *Primitives* (New York: Beacon, 1927), p. 98.

94. C. Reagan, '1855–1848: Lessons for Today', *The Irish Reporter* (1995), Volume 19.

95. Marcel Mauss, *Sacrifice: Its Nature and Function* (New York: Knopf, 1964).

96. G. Steadman-Jones, *Outcast London* (London: Peregrine, 1987), p. 252.

97. A. Court, *Puck of the Droms*, p. 56.

98. Jim Mac Laughlin, 'Isolation reduces Travellers to social outcasts', *The Irish Times*, January 7, 1995 ; P. Yeates, 'Christmas influx widens the cultural divide', *The Irish Times* (January 7, 1995).

99. Michael Ignatieff, *Blood and Belonging: Journeys in the New Nationalism* (London: Vintage, 1993).

100. Jim Mac Laughlin, 'Defending the Frontiers' (1993), p. 39.

101. Jim Mac Laughlin, 'The Geography of Closure and anti-Traveller Racism', *Chimera*, University College Cork Geographical Journal, 1994, pp. 131–35.

102. Hanafin, 'Go, Move, Shift', p. 7.

103. Mc Veigh, 'Irish Racism' (1992), p. 43.

104. Belfast Traveller Support Group, *Briefing Document on Travellers for the Committee on the Administration of Justice* (Belfast, 1991), p. 5.

105. Mc Veigh, 'Irish Racism', p. 45.

106. Niall Crowley 'Racism and Travellers' in *Anti-racism Law and the Travellers* (1993), p.15.

107. Quoted in Mc Veigh, 'Irish Racism,' p. 44.

108. Derek Hawes and Barbara Perez, *The Gypsy and the State: The Ethnic Cleansing of British Society* (Bristol: Bristol University School for Advanced Urban Studies, 1994).

109. Niall Crowley, 'Racism and Travellers'.

110. Balibar and Wallerstein, *Race and Nation* (1991), p. 47.

111. Susannah Ward, 'Romanies: 1000 years on the road', *Focus Magazine* (April 1995), pp. 84–9.

112. Patricia Redlitch, 'Profoundly dishonest, and we're not talking about the itinerants', *Sunday Independent* (February 19, 1995).

113. Ibid.

114. Crowley, 'Racism and Travellers, p. 17.

115. Will Hanafin, 'Go, Move, Shift', p. 8.

116. Antonio Gramsci, *Selections from the Prison Notebooks* (London: Lawrence and Wishart, 1971), pp. 44–55.

117. M. Cummins, 'Traveller question must be faced and not avoided', *The Irish Times* (November 12, 1994).